Nick
LeForce
343-3435

EXERCISES IN HELPING SKILLS

A Training Manual
to Accompany THE SKILLED HELPER

EXERCISES IN HELPING SKILLS

A Training Manual
to Accompany THE SKILLED HELPER

by GERARD EGAN

Loyola University of Chicago

BROOKS/COLE PUBLISHING COMPANY
MONTEREY, CALIFORNIA
A DIVISION OF WADSWORTH PUBLISHING COMPANY, INC.

ISBN: 0-8185-0146-4

Printed in the United States of America

10 9 8 7 6 5 4 3

CONTENTS

EXERCISES IN HELPING SKILLS

**A Training Manual
to Accompany THE SKILLED HELPER**

INTRODUCTION

The exercises in this manual are meant to accompany *The Skilled Helper* by Gerard Egan (Brooks/Cole Publishing Company, Monterey, California, 1975). The purpose of these exercises is to help the trainee begin to translate into practice the skills of the developmental helping model outlined in *The Skilled Helper*. Since helping is an art, it demands practice on the part of the trainee—practice in all of the skills of the model. The trainee can prepare for practice with his fellow trainees in the training group, first, by gaining a cognitive understanding of the model and its skills (through reading and lectures) and, second, by seeing these skills modeled by a teacher or trainer. Most of the exercises in this manual give the trainee the opportunity to practice the helping skills privately, in writing, before practicing them publicly, in actual helping interchanges with his fellow trainees. In a sense, the trainee practices on himself before practicing on others. These exercises help the trainee clarify, behaviorally, his understanding of the helping skills; therefore, they prepare him more immediately for one-to-one practice in these skills. They provide a behavioral link between a theoretical understanding of the skills and their actual practice. Although these exercises can in no way substitute for actual practice in helping, they can be useful in broadening courses that ordinarily deal only with the theory of helping.

The order of exercises here generally follows the order in which the skills are presented in *The Skilled Helper* (see Table 1 for a summary of the stages of the developmental model and the stage-specific skills).

The exercises in this manual relate to attending behavior and to the first two stages of the three-stage developmental model of helping. The omission of Stage III in no way implies that action programs are unimportant, for, indeed, effective helping culminates in constructive behavioral change. The best exercise I have found for trainees in Stage III is to work systematically through the self-directed change program outlined in Watson and Tharp's *Self-Directed Behavior* (Brooks/Cole Publishing Company, Monterey, California, 1973). This book provides a solid basic understanding of the principles underlying the maintenance and change of human behavior. It has the trainee translate these principles into practice in a systematic self-change program. The trainee practices on himself, as it were, before trying to help others. The trainees share their self-modification projects as they move through them during the helper-training program. They have an opportunity to use the Stage-I and Stage-II skills they are learning to help one another on the self-change projects. If the helper-training program is an extensive one, I have the trainees undertake a second self-modification project, using the force-field analysis approach to problem-solving presented under Stage III in *The Skilled Helper*. Again, the trainees use the Stage-I and Stage-II skills they are learning to help one another in these projects. This manual is a working tool and, like the developmental model of helping itself, is open to modification and development to suit the needs of trainees and the training program.

Table 1

The developmental (three-stage) model of helping is a commonsense "folk" model. Its basic form is: *"Think. Judge. Act."*

THE CLIENT: This model sets sequential tasks for the client in the helping process:

I. Explore your behavior.   II. Seek action-oriented self-understanding.   III. Act on these understandings. Examine your problems.   "Own" the consequences of self-exploration.

THE HELPER: the phases of the model demand various helper *skills*:

PRE-HELPING

attending physically
attending psychologically

I. RESPONDING (to the client's frame of reference)

primary accurate empathy
concreteness
respect
genuineness

II. STIMULATING (the client to alternative frames of reference)

advanced accurate empathy
self-disclosure
confrontation
immediacy

III. HELPING TO ACT

problem-solving techniques
behavioral strategies
action programs

This is a HELPER-TRAINING model:

Helpers are trained systematically in all of the skills listed above. Personal-growth issues constitute the *content* of the practice helping interactions.

This is a TRAINING-AS-TREATMENT model:

The clients are trained systematically and directly in the skills of the model ("life" skills). The problematic real-life issues of client-trainees constitute the *content* of practice sessions.

This is a GROUP-ORIENTED model: the preferred mode of training is in groups.

It is an OPEN, INTEGRATING model:

It is open to change or development; its goal is to meet the needs of clients and helpers. It is *systematic* but not school-oriented. It is eclectic, borrowing systematically from all schools and systems. Its major bases are: skills training, social-influence theory, and the principles and techniques of behavioral change.

3

SECTION 1
PREPARATION FOR PLAYING THE ROLE OF CLIENT IN HELPING INTERACTIONS

Exercise 1: Appropriate self-disclosure for trainees: A search for themes

As a trainee, you are going to be asked to act both as a helper and as a client in practice sessions. Even in the written exercises in this manual, you are asked to play these two roles. When you play the role of client, what should you talk about? There are two general possibilities:

1. you can role-play—that is, pretend to have certain problems, or
2. you can discuss your own real problems.

Role-playing, although not easy, is still less personally demanding than discussing your own problems in practice sessions. However, although some role-playing might be useful at the beginning of the training process (since it is less threatening and allows you to ease yourself into the role of client), you should eventually use the training process to look at real problems in your own life, especially those problems or characteristics of interpersonal style that interfere with your effectiveness as a helper. For instance, if you are an impatient person—one who places unreasonable demands on others—you will have to examine and change this behavior if you want to become an effective helper. If you deal with your own problems during the training program, you will get a feeling for what it means to be a helpee in a way that is impossible through mere role-playing. I'm sure that most of us would prefer to go to a helper who has learned in an experiential way what goes on inside a person who is seeking help.

However, if you are to talk about yourself during the practice sessions, you should take some care in choosing what you are going to reveal about yourself. This exercise is meant to help you review possible topics to use during practice sessions. Careful execution of this exercise will give you a list of problems that are neither too superficial nor too intimate for the training group. Without preparation, you can find yourself talking about things that are not really problematic (or problems that have long been solved) or talking about things you had no intention of revealing. As you build rapport with your fellow trainees and learn to trust one another more deeply (and trust one another's

4

developing skills), you can move from role-playing to dealing with simpler personal problems to dealing with more substantive issues.

Self-disclosure, however, should always remain appropriate to the goals of training. The purpose of this exercise is not to force you into "secret-dropping" or into dramatic self-disclosure. In fact, it is meant to help you avoid that. Although it is true that an effective helper is a person who deals directly with the problems of his life as they come up, the person who is training to be a helper should still decide—in conjunction with the teacher or trainer, if necessary—which problems are appropriate to the training forum and which problems should be handled in some other forum.

This exercise should also help you choose problem areas that are capable of some extended development, so that you can avoid having to find a new problem every time you assume the role of client.

Below is a limited sample of the kinds of problems or characteristics of interpersonal style that might serve as the content of practice sessions.

I'm shy. My shyness takes the form of being afraid to meet strangers and of being afraid to reveal myself to others.

I'm not assertive enough. Others can run roughshod over me and I just "take it."

I get angry very easily and let my anger spill out on others in irresponsible ways. I think my anger is often linked to my not getting my own way.

I'm a lazy person. I find it especially difficult to expend the kind of energy necessary to listen to and get involved with others.

I'm somewhat fearful of persons of the opposite sex. This is especially true if I get the feeling that they want some kind of intimacy with me. I get nervous and tongue-tied.

I'm a rather insensitive person. I find it hard to know what others are feeling. I'm the bull-in-the-china-shop type.

I'm overly controlled. I don't let my emotions show at all, if possible. Sometimes I don't want them to show even to myself.

I like to control others, but I like to do so in subtle ways. I want to stay in charge of interpersonal situations at all times.

I have a need to be liked by others. I seldom do anything that might offend others, because I have a need to be seen as a good guy.

I have no positive feelings about myself. In general, I think of myself as inferior and sometimes even as "no good."

I never stop to examine my value system. I think I hold some conflicting values. I'm not even sure why I'm interested in helping others.

I feel almost compelled to help others. I get nervous when I'm not engaged in helping. People with problems are almost necessary for me.

I'm very sensitive, easily hurt. I send out messages to others that say "Be careful of me."

In a number of ways, I am a dependent person. My self-image depends too much on how others see me.

I am a counterdependent person. I always have to show others that I'm free and an individual in my own right. I find it difficult to get along with others, especially those in authority.

I'm an overly anxious person, especially in interpersonal situations. But I don't know why I'm like that.

I am, at least relatively, a colorless, uninteresting person. I'm bored with myself at times and assume that others are bored with me.

I take too many irresponsible risks in interpersonal situations. I'm rash and impulsive. I lack adequate self-control.

I'm stubborn and pig-headed. I'm very opinionated, and I'm ready to argue with almost anyone on anything. This puts people off.

I'm somewhat sneaky and devious in my relationships with others. I seduce people in various ways (not necessarily sexual) by my charm. I get them to do what I want.

I have little or no investment in examining my interpersonal style in any depth. I'm content with things the way they are.

I'm very materialistic and heavily invested in my own personal comfort. I think that what I want is the good life, and I fear that caring about people might be secondary.

I feel socially inept at times. I don't do the right—the human—thing at the right time. For instance, I don't notice when others are suffering some emotion and, as a result, I seem to be callous.

There is a degree of loneliness in my life. I don't think others like me. I spend a great deal of time feeling sorry for myself.

I'm stingy. With money and with time. I don't want to share what I have.

I feel a bit "out of it," for I believe that I'm inexperienced and somewhat naive. When others talk about their experiences, I feel apprehensive or left out, or I find it hard to get a feeling for what they mean. I've led too sheltered a life.

I'm somewhat of a coward. I find it hard to stand up for my convictions when I meet even light opposition. It's easy to get me to retreat.

I find it hard to face conflict when I see it between myself and someone else, or even when others are in conflict. I get scared. I run from it. I'm more or less a peace-at-any-price person.

When I am confronted, even legitimately and responsibly, I tend to attack my confronter and to respond in other defensive ways.

This list is not exhaustive. It is meant to help stimulate your thinking about yourself in ways related to the goals of training. Below, briefly list as many of your dissatisfactions, problems, and unused personal resources as possible.

1. _I feel unable to make satisfactory plans for the future, both emotionally & materially_

2. _I sometimes find it difficult to assert my interests, interpersonally particularly_

3. _____

_____

4. _____

_____

5. _____

_____

6. _____

   _____

7. _____

   _____

8. _____

   _____

9. _____

   _____

10. _____

   _____

11. _____

   _____

12. _____

   _____

13. _____

   _____

14. _____

   _____

15. _____

   _____

16. _____

   _____

17. _____

   _____

18. _____

   _____

19. _____

   _____

20. _____

_____

21. _____

_____

22. _____

_____

23. _____

_____

24. _____

_____

25. _____

_____

26. _____

_____

27. _____

_____

28. _____

_____

Choose the issues you wish to discuss.

X   Mark an X through the numbers of the issues you think are too intimate to discuss, issues that are not appropriate for the training group (or for this stage), or issues you simply don't want to discuss.

( )   Place parentheses around the numbers of the issues that you think you might be willing to discuss in the practice sessions.

H   Place an H in front of the numbers of the issues you think might affect your functioning as a helper.

T   Place a T in front of the numbers of those issues you believe are capable of some thematic development— that is, problem areas or areas of concern that might be explored at some length.

Obviously, as the training program moves forward, you might want to add other issues or change your mind regarding the issues you do or do not want to talk about. The purpose of this exercise is to help you discover some substantive areas that you feel relatively comfortable discussing.

An Example

A trainee's list could look something like this:

T (1.) I'm intellectually lazy; I don't use my intellectual resources well.

H T X I am an elitist, and I've refrained from confronting or exploring my prejudices.

T X I'm sexually immature.

T H X I am an opportunist, and I'm manipulative in many ways.

(5.) I'm somewhat overweight.

T H X I am seductive in various ways.

T H (7.) I'm selfish in many ways.

T X I think I should get involved in social-change movements, but I don't do much about it.

T H (9.) I sometimes shirk responsibility in favor of personal comfort and satisfaction.

T (10.) I'm very fickle in my likes and dislikes.

T (11.) I fail to review my values from time to time to determine just what my operative values are.

H (12.) I'm shy and uncomfortable in situations in which I feel threatened by those more intelligent and articulate than I.

T X I've had a falling-out with my father.

T H (14.) I often find myself bored with people and things.

Some of this trainee's judgments might change over the course of the training period. For instance, as trust develops within the training group, he may feel that he could appropriately include more intimate issues. However, the trainee should be in command of his own self-disclosure and should not be pressured by others. Each trainee's list should provide him with some "T-H-( )" areas with which to start with relative comfort.

SECTION 2
ATTENDING

EXERCISES IN PHYSICAL ATTENDING

These exercises deal with the way you use your body to communicate with another person. Before doing these exercises, review the chapter on attending in *The Skilled Helper*. Recall especially the basic elements of physical attending:

S—face the other person SQUARELY

O—adopt an OPEN posture

L—LEAN toward the other

E—keep good EYE contact

R—try to be "at home" or relatively RELAXED in this position

Exercise 2: Experiencing nonattending in a one-to-one conversation

1. Choose a partner from among the members of your training group.
2. Partner A should adopt an attending position; Partner B should violate the rules of attending (he should *not* face his partner squarely, and so on).
3. Conduct a three- or four-minute discussion of your goals for this training experience, what you would like to accomplish, and so forth.
4. After four minutes or so, change roles so that Partner A now violates the rules of good attending while Partner B assumes an attending position. Continue the conversation on goals for another three or four minutes.
5. Stop the conversation and process how you felt in both attending and nonattending positions, what impact the other's attending or nonattending had on you, and so on.

Exercise 3: Experiencing nonattending in a group conversation

1. Have all the members of the training group (six to eight members) meet in a circle for a group discussion.
2. Choose a topic related to training (for example, what fears you have as you move into the training experience).
3. Have a discussion of the topic for three or four minutes, during which half of the members attend while the other half assume various nonattending positions.
4. After three or four minutes, the nonattenders now attend, while the attenders now assume various nonattending positions.
5. Stop the discussion and discuss the effects of attending and non-attending as concretely as possible.

Exercise 4: Degrees of attending in a one-to-one conversation

1. Choose a partner from among the members of your training group. Your partner will act as "client."
2. Choose a topic of conversation related to training.
3. Start the conversation in a minimally attending position.
4. At a signal from the trainer, move into an intensely attending position. Continue for another two or three minutes.
5. Stop the conversation and discuss the different effects of differ-ent degrees of attending, from the viewpoints of both the one com-municating and the one being communicated to.

Exercise 5: Degrees of attending in a group conversation

1. Have all the members of the training group meet in a circle for a group discussion.
2. Continue discussing the topic from Exercise 2 above.
3. In the beginning, the members should assume only minimally attending positions, but all should attend.
4. After a few minutes of discussion, at a signal from the trainer, all the members should move to intense attending positions. Continue the conversation for another few minutes.
5. Stop the conversation and discuss the differences felt between minimal and intense attending positions.

Exercise 6: Listening to nonverbal and paralinguistic cues

Physical attending has two functions: (1) it is a sign to the other that I am actively present and working with him, and (2) it helps me to be an *active listener* (that is, my physical attending helps my psycho-logical attending). To what do I listen? I listen to both the verbal and the nonverbal messages of the person with whom I am talking. The purpose of this exercise is to become more sensitive to nonverbal and paralinguistic cues and messages. ("Paralinguistic" refers to the way one uses one's voice in the communication process; paralinguistic cues include tone of voice, loudness, pitch, pacing of words, stumbling over words, grunts, sighs, and so on.) Nonverbal and paralinguistic cues have two general functions: (1) they confirm, punctuate, emphasize, modulate, or otherwise modify the verbal messages of the speaker; or, sometimes, (2) they contradict the verbal message of the speaker and thus contain the real message. For instance, if the speaker raises his voice and pounds on the table while delivering an angry message, then both raising the voice (a paralinguistic cue) and pounding on the table (a nonverbal behavior) underscore and emphasize his anger. However, if the speaker says in a very hesitating way (a paralinguistic cue) and while fidgeting with his hands (a nonverbal cue) that yes, he would like to go out to dinner that night, then the nonverbal and paralinguistic cues contain the real message, one that contradicts the verbal message.

Directions

Trainees should divide into groups of four (Members A, B, C, and D). Members A and B should spend five or six minutes discussing what they like and don't like about their present interpersonal styles (or any other topic relevant to the training experience). Members C and D act as observers. While A and B are speaking, C and D should take written notes on A's and B's nonverbal and paralinguistic behavior. The speakers' behavior should be observed and noted, but C and D should take care not to overinterpret this behavior. After five or six minutes, C and D should give A and B feedback on the highlights of their nonverbal and paralinguistic behavior. Then roles should be switched and the process repeated, with A and B becoming the observers and C and D the interactants.

Samples of typical feedback statements

"Most of the time you spoke very quickly, in spurts. It gave me a feeling of tension or nervousness."

"You sat very still throughout the dialogue. Your hands remained folded in your lap the whole time, and there was practically no bodily movement. It made you look very 'proper.' It gave me an impression of shyness or rigidity."

"When you talked about being a very sensitive person, one who is easily hurt, you began to stumble over your words a bit. The message seemed to be that you are sensitive about being so sensitive."

"You tapped your left foot almost constantly."

"You put your hand to your mouth a great deal. It gave me the impression of hesitancy on your part."

"When B began talking hesitatingly about being shy, you leaned back and even moved your chair back a bit. I'm not sure whether you were showing that he made you uncomfortable, or whether you were easing off, giving him room to speak."

"You broke eye contact a great deal when you were talking about yourself, but not when you were listening."

"You were so relaxed—at times you even slouched a bit—that you almost gave me the impression that you were uninterested in the whole task."

A caution

The purpose of this exercise is to make you aware of nonverbal and paralinguistic cues. At this stage, you should begin to note the amount and variety of such behavior, but be slow to interpret such behavior. As you gradually become more aware of nonverbal and paralinguistic behavior, your abilities to interpret and to read these cues intelligently will grow with your experience. However, great care should be taken to interpret such behavior only within the *total* communication context (which includes who is talking to whom, under what circumstances, with what antecedents, on what topics, and so on). Sometimes the same nonverbal behavior can mean different things depending on the total communication context. For instance, a drooping head and a stony expression can mean dejection or anger or despair, but such behavior does not *invariably* indicate any of these. Finally, if you become overly preoccupied with nonverbal and paralinguistic cues and their interpretation, you will become overly self-conscious about the communication process itself. Obviously, such self-consciousness is self-defeating.

Exercise 7: Attending to verbal messages: An exercise in parroting

There is a great difference between parroting back to a person what he has said and communicating to him with accurate empathy that you have understood, from his frame of reference, what he has said. However, accurate empathy does depend, in part, on your ability to attend to and remember the substance of the other's verbal messages. Therefore, this is an exercise in parroting—the ability merely to repeat back to the speaker what he has said to you. Later on, the substantial differences between parroting and communicating accurate empathy will be emphasized.

Directions

Trainees should be divided into groups of three: a communicator, a listener, and an observer.

1. The communicator makes a statement about himself, but limits his statement to one (complex) sentence.
2. The listener uses the formula: "You said that . . ." and repeats the substance of what the communicator has said.
3. The observer, who may jot down written notes to help him in his task, then gives the listener feedback on his accuracy. The feedback should be very brief and should indicate what the listener has left out, if anything.

4. The same process is repeated, except that the communicator makes two statements about himself.
5. The same process is repeated, except that the communicator makes three statements about himself.
6. Finally, the entire process (steps 1 through 5) is repeated for each member of the triad (so that each has the opportunity to be listener, communicator, and observer).

SECTION 3
CONCRETENESS

EXERCISES IN CONCRETENESS

If you are to help others to speak concretely about themselves, you must first learn what concreteness is and how to speak concretely about yourself. Before doing the following exercises, review the sections on concreteness in *The Skilled Helper*.

Concreteness means speaking about specific *experiences* ("experience" here refers to what happens to me, what others do to me), speaking about specific *behaviors* ("behavior" here means what I do), and speaking about specific *feelings* (that accompany my experiences and my behavior).

Exercise 8: Speaking concretely about experiences

In the following exercise, you are asked to speak about some of your experiences—first vaguely, then concretely.

Study the following examples.

Example 1

Vague statement of experience: "Things were not so hot today."
Concrete statement of experience: "I had a headache for several hours while I was at work this morning."

Example 2

Vague statement of experience: "People pick on me."
Concrete statement of experience: "My classmates ridicule me for being fat. They call me 'Porky' and 'Tubby.' They don't invite me to their parties. They even say they don't invite me because I'd eat too much."

In the spaces below, deal with five instances of your own experience. Stick to experiences in the sense defined above; don't include feelings

15

and/or behaviors. Try to choose experiences, negative or positive, that are relevant to your interpersonal style and to the training experience.

1. a. Vague _____

_____

   b. Concrete _____

_____

_____

_____

_____

2. a. Vague _____

_____

   b. Concrete _____

_____

_____

_____

3. a. Vague _____

_____

   b. Concrete _____

_____

_____

_____

4. a. Vague _____

_____

   b. Concrete _____

_____

_____

_____

5. a. Vague _____

_____

b.   Concrete _____

_____

_____

_____

_____

Exercise 9: Speaking concretely about behavior

In the following exercise, you are asked to speak about some of your behaviors (what you do or fail to do)—first vaguely, then concretely.
Study the following examples.

Example 1

Vague statement of behavior: "I tend to mess things up sometimes."
Concrete statement of behavior: "I went away last weekend and did no studying or writing. As a result, I failed a test on Monday, and I might not get my term paper in on time."

Example 2

Vague statement of behavior: "I don't treat my wife right."
Concrete statement of behavior: "When I come home from work, I read the paper and communicate very little with my wife. I don't share what went right or what went wrong at the office. Neither do I encourage her to talk about what has happened to her. Still, if I feel like having sex later, I expect her to hop in bed with me."

In the spaces below, deal with five instances of your own behavior. Stick to behaviors rather than describing feelings and/or experiences. Try to choose behaviors that are relevant to your interpersonal style and/or to your helping style—that is, relevant to the training experience.

1.   a.   Vague _____

_____

b.   Concrete _____

_____

_____

_____

_____

2. a. Vague _____

_____

b. Concrete _____

_____

_____

_____

_____

3. a. Vague _____

_____

b. Concrete _____

_____

_____

_____

_____

4. a. Vague _____

_____

b. Concrete _____

_____

_____

_____

_____

5. a. Vague _____

_____

b. Concrete _____

_____

_____

_____

_____

Exercise 10: Speaking concretely about feelings

In the following exercise, you are asked to speak about some of your feelings: first vaguely, then concretely. Feelings should be related to the concrete experiences or behaviors that underlie or cause them.

Study the following examples.

Example 1 (feelings related to behavior)

Vague statement of feelings: "Training groups give me a hard time."
Concrete statement of feelings: "I feel hesitant and embarrassed whenever I try to say what I think to another member of our training group."

Example 2 (feelings related to experience)

Vague statement of feelings: "My relationship with my mother bothers me sometimes."
Concrete statement of feelings: "I feel guilty and depressed whenever my mother calls and says she's lonely. She called twice this week."

In the spaces below, deal with five instances of your own feelings. As in the examples above, relate these feelings either to your experience or to your behavior. Try to formulate examples whose content is relevant to your interpersonal and/or helping style and to this training experience.

1. a. Vague _____

    _____

    b. Concrete _____

    _____

    _____

    _____

    _____

2. a. Vague _____

    _____

    b. Concrete _____

    _____

    _____

    _____

    _____

3. a. Vague _____

    _____

    b. Concrete _____

    _____

    _____

    _____

    _____

4. a. Vague _____

    _____

    b. Concrete _____

    _____

    _____

    _____

    _____

5. a. Vague _____

    _____

    b. Concrete _____

    _____

    _____

    _____

    _____

Exercise 11: Speaking concretely about experiences, behaviors, and feelings together

    In this exercise, you are asked to bring together all three elements—specific experiences, specific behaviors, and specific feelings—in talking about yourself.
    Study the following examples.

Example 1

Vague statement: "People turn me off at times."
Concrete statement: "I feel small and inept when my two roommates brag about their accomplishments when we're all together. I clam up, and then I feel even more alone and miserable."

Pick out the feelings, the experiences, and the behaviors in this example.

Example 2

Vague statement: "Things went okay between you and me in today's training session."
Concrete statement: "I felt encouraged this afternoon because you spoke to me directly three or four times. The edge in your voice seemed to be missing, and that made me more comfortable. The couple of times I found the courage to give you feedback on your helping style, I felt elated because you accepted it."

Pick out the feelings, the experiences, and the behaviors in this example.

In the spaces below, first make a general or vague statement about yourself and your behavior, and then transform it into a statement with specific experiences, feelings, and behaviors. Try to make your statements relevant to your interpersonal and/or helping style and to the training experience itself.

1. a. Vague _____

    _____

    b. Concrete _____

        _____

        _____

        _____

        _____

        _____

2. a. Vague _____

    _____

b.   Concrete _____

_____

_____

_____

_____

_____

_____

SECTION 4
THE COMPONENT PARTS OF PRIMARY-LEVEL ACCURATE EMPATHY

THE TRAINEE: THE EXPERIENCING AND THE LANGUAGE OF EMOTION

If you are to help others clarify their feelings and emotions, you must be in touch with your own emotions and have at your fingertips a vocabulary that is expressive of emotion. The following exercises focus on the language of emotion and your experiencing of emotion.

Exercise 12: Expanding one's facility in expressing feelings and emotions

Feelings and emotions can be expressed in a variety of ways.

By single words:

    I feel good.
    I'm angry.
    I feel caught.
    I feel abandoned.
    I'm depressed.
    I'm delighted.

By phrases (idiomatic, idiosyncratic, descriptive, metaphorical):

    I'm out of sorts.
    I've got my back against the wall.
    I'm sitting on top of the world.
    I'm down in the dumps.

Through the implications of experiential and behavioral statements:

Experiential statements (what is happening to me):

    I feel I'm being dumped on.
    I feel she loves me.

I feel I'm being scrutinized, evaluated, and stereotyped.
I feel he cares.

Behavioral statements (what action I feel like taking):

I feel like giving up.
I feel like hugging you.
I feel like telling them off.
I feel like singing and dancing through the streets.

Note that feelings and emotions are expressed through implication (and therefore indirectly) in experiential and behavioral statements.

I feel bad   because I'm being dumped on.

"I feel bad" is, in a sense, more direct; that is, it describes the primary emotional state directly. However, experiential and behavioral statements of emotion are often more colorful and dramatic and therefore, in their own way, more direct than mere statements of primary emotions. Experiential and behavioral statements of emotion often refer, in word-economical ways, to both feelings and *content*. Therefore, in the statement

"I feel she loves me"

the implication is

"I feel great" (*primary emotional state*)
"because I think she loves me" (*content—that is, experience
                                   underlying the feeling*).

The purpose of this exercise is to help you expand the ways in which you express feelings and emotions.

A wide variety of affective states are listed below. You are to express them in all four of the ways indicated above. In the first part of the exercise, you will be given an example in each affective category. Then you will do one of your own.

1. *Joy*

Single word: I'm happy.
Phrase: I'm on cloud nine.
Experiential statement: I feel he likes my work.
Behavioral statement: I feel like going out to dinner to celebrate.

Now do one of your own in the same category: *joy*.

Single word: —————————————————————————————————

Phrase: ————————————————————————————————————

Experiential statement: ——————————————————————————

——

Behavioral statement: _____

_____

2. *Anger*

    Single word: I'm annoyed.
    Phrase: I'm out of sorts.
    Experiential statement: I feel I'm getting a raw deal.
    Behavioral statement: I feel like telling them off.

Now do one of your own in the same category: *anger*.

Single word: _____

Phrase: _____

Experiential statement: _____

_____

Behavioral statement: _____

_____

3. *Anxiety*

    Single word: I'm nervous.
    Phrase: I'm on pins and needles.
    Experiential statement: I feel he's scrutinizing and judging me.
    Behavioral statement: I feel like jumping out of my skin.

Single word: _____

Phrase: _____

Experiential statement: _____

_____

Behavioral statement: _____

_____

4. *Shame, embarrassment*

    Single word: I feel naked.
    Phrase: I feel like two cents.
    Experiential: I feel I've been unmasked.
    Behavioral: I feel like crawling under a rock.

Single word: _____

Phrase: _____

Experiential: _____

_____

Behavioral: _____

_____

5. *Defeat*

   Single word: I feel destroyed.
   Phrase: I feel done for.
   Experiential: I feel he's got me cornered.
   Behavioral: I feel like throwing in the towel.

Single word: _____

Phrase: _____

Experiential: _____

_____

Behavioral: _____

_____

For the following affective states, use a single word, a phrase, and either an experiential *or* a behavioral statement.

6. *Confusion*

Single word: _____

Phrase: _____

Experiential/behavioral: _____

_____

7. *Guilt, regret*

Single word: _____

Phrase: _____

Experiential/behavioral: _____

_____

8. *Rejection*

Single word: _____

Phrase: _____

Experiential/behavioral: _____

_____

9. *Depression*

Single word: _____

Phrase: _____

Experiential/behavioral: _____

_____

10. *Peace*

Single word: _____

Phrase: _____

Experiential/behavioral: _____

_____

11. *Pressure*

Single word: _____

Phrase: _____

Experiential/behavioral: _____

_____

12. *Capability, competence*

Single word: _____

Phrase: _____

Experiential/behavioral: _____

_____

13. *Low self-esteem*

Single word: _____

Phrase: _____

Experiential/behavioral: _____

_____

14. *Satisfaction*

Single word: _____

Phrase: _____

Experiential/behavioral: _____

_____

15. *Misused, abused*

Single word: _____

Phrase: _____

Experiential/behavioral: _____

_____

16. *Low physical energy*

Single word: _____

Phrase: _____

Experiential/behavioral: _____

_____

17. *Affliction, distress*

Single word: _____

Phrase: _____

Experiential/behavioral: _____

_____

18. *Loving*

Single word: _____

Phrase: _____

Experiential/behavioral: _____

_____

19. *Constrained, hindered*

Single word: _____

Phrase: _____

Experiential/behavioral: _____

_____

20. *Boredom*

Single word: _____

Phrase: _____

Experiential/behavioral: _____

_____

21. *Hope*

Single word: _____

Phrase: _____

Experiential/behavioral: _____

_____

Exercise 13: A review of feelings and emotions

If you are to help others clarify their feelings and emotions, you should first be familiar with your own emotional states. In *How Do You Feel?*, edited by John Wood (Prentice-Hall, Inc., Englewood Cliffs, New Jersey, 1974), Wood and others describe in some detail their own experience of a wide variety of emotional states. These emotional states are listed below. You are asked to describe what you feel when you feel these emotions. Describe what you feel as *concretely* as possible:

How does your body react? What happens inside you? What do you feel like doing?

Read the following examples before doing this exercise.

Example 1

Accepted: When I feel accepted,

I feel warm inside.
I feel safe.
I feel free to be myself.
I feel I can let my guard down.
I feel like sharing myself.
I feel my strengths more deeply.
Some of my fears ease away.
I feel at home.
I feel at peace.
I feel some residues of loneliness drain away.

Example 2

Scared: When I feel scared,

My mouth dries up.
My bowels become loose.
There are butterflies in my stomach.
I feel like running away.
I feel the need to talk to someone understanding.
I'm unable to concentrate.
I turn in on myself.
I feel extremely vulnerable.
Sometimes I feel like crying out.

This should not be just an intellectual exercise. *Try to picture yourself in situations in which you have actually experienced these emotions.* Then write down what you see in your imagination. You will need **extra paper to do this exercise.**

Part I

The emotions: When I feel

1. accepted	11. defensive	22. lonely
2. affectionate	12. disappointed	23. loving
3. afraid	13. free	24. rejected
4. angry	14. frustrated	25. repulsed
5. anxious	15. guilty	26. respect
6. attracted	16. hopeful	27. sad
7. bored	17. hurt	28. satisfied
8. that I belong (community)	18. inferior	29. shy
	19. intimate	30. suspicious
9. competitive	20. jealous	31. superior
10. confused	21. joyful	32. trusting

Once you have described how you feel when you feel all of these emotions, you should have a wider repertory of words, phrases, and behavioral and experiential statements, both to describe your own emotional states as they arise and to identify them in others.

Part 2

This time, review these same emotions. Can you recall an intense or memorable experience in which each of these emotions played an important part? When was this experience? With whom? How intense?

Example

Scared: "I was going to Europe last year by plane. The captain told us that it would be a smooth flight. About an hour and a half after take-off, it was as if we hit a brick wall. For the next three hours, we jumped and bumped and dived and swooped up. No one said anything to us. People began to get sick. I didn't realize that I could experience terror for three hours straight. I didn't talk to anyone. I was just this huge jangle of nerves for over three hours."

Part 3

Review the list once more. Identify the emotional areas that you find problematic. Use this list to expand, add to, clarify, and concretize the problems listed in Exercise 1.

THE DISCRIMINATION OF FEELINGS AND OF CONTENT

The next four exercises (14 to 17) deal with the *discrimination* of feelings and of content. At this point, review the distinction between discrimination and communication in *The Skilled Helper*.

Exercise 14: The passive discrimination of feelings

Directions

Circle the adjectives that accurately identify the speaker's *feelings* in the following statements.

1. "These counseling sessions have really done me a great deal of good. I enjoy my work more. I actually look forward to meeting new people. My husband and I are talking more directly and seriously and decently to each other. There's just so much more freedom in my life!"

This person feels

a. awful   b. good   c. uncertain   d. cautious   e. great

f. moody   g. on top of the world   h. perplexed   i. excited

j. delighted   k. alive

2. "My husband and I just decided to get a divorce. (*Pause*) I really don't look forward to the legal part of it—to *any* part of it. And, to tell you the truth, I just don't know what to expect. (*Pause*) I'm well into middle age. I don't think another marriage is possible. (*Pause*) I just don't know what to expect."

This person feels

a. assured   b. depressed   c. pleased   d. sad   e. brave

f. downcast   g. discouraged   h. worried   i. strong

3. "My best friend has just turned her back on me. And I don't even know why. From the way she acted, I think she thinks I've been talking behind her back. Damn! This neighborhood is full of gossips. I hope she hasn't been listening to those foulmouths who just want to stir up trouble."

This person feels

a. angry   b. elated   c. put out   d. enthusiastic

e. congenial   f. confident   g. agitated   h. confused

4. "My teacher told me today that I've done better work than she ever expected. I always thought that I could be good at studies if I really tried. So I risked it this semester, and it paid off."

This person feels

a. disillusioned   b. vengeful   c. skeptical   d. competent

e. successful   f. unsure   g. patient   h. gratified

i. jealous   j. tolerant   k. cautious   l. annoyed

5. "I should never have allowed my daughter to go to the movies alone. I don't know what my wife will say when she gets home from work. She says I'm careless—but being careless with the kids—that's something else. I almost feel as if *I* had broken Karen's arm, not the guy in that car."

This person feels

a. relieved   b. confident   c. guilty   d. arrogant

e. miserable   f. ashamed   g. apprehensive   h. spiteful

i. angry with himself   j. loving   k. anxious

6. "I've been in college two years now, and nothing much has happened. The teachers here are only so-so. And you can't say that the social life around here is much. Things go on the same from day to day, week after week."

This person feels

a. shocked   b. relaxed   c. on a plateau   d. empty   e. pleased

f. blah   g. bored   h. listless   i. indignant

7. "I've finally met a woman who is very genuine and who lets me be myself. I can care about her deeply without making a child out of her. And she cares about me without mothering me. It's a good, solid feeling. We've been thinking about getting married."

This person feels

a. loved   b. whimsical   c. listless   d. at peace

e. genuine   f. honest   g. doubtful   h. put upon

i. content   j. overlooked   k. tired

8. "Why does my husband keep blaming me for his trouble with the kids? I'm always in the middle. He complains to me about them. They complain to me about him. I could walk right out on the whole thing. Who the hell do they think they are?"

This person feels

a. empty   b. jubilant   c. resentful   d. cornered   e. angry

f. inferior   g. tough   h. "damned if I do, damned if I don't"

i. picked on   j. ignored   k. alive

9. "I [a group trainee] don't know what to expect from this group. I've never been in a group before. I get the feeling that the rest of you are pros, so I'm afraid that I won't do what's right. I want to learn how to be a helper, but I'm not sure I can do that in this group."

33

This person feels

a. afraid　　b. inadequate　c. uncomfortable　d. inferior

e. humiliated　f. forceful　g. moody　　h. hesitant

i. spiteful　j. anxious　　k. insecure　　l. mellow

10. "I [a client] don't know what I'm doing here. You're the third
counselor they've sent me to—or is it the fourth? None of them
did anything for me. In fact, I've never been interested. Why do
they keep making me come here? It's just a waste of your time and
a waste of mine. Let's just fold the show right now."

This person feels

a. alarmed　b. at ease　c. rejected　d. competent　e. reluctant

f. awed　　g. under the weather　h. loathed　i. discouraged

j. cocky　k. it's futile　l. agreeable　m. well-meaning

Exercise 15: The passive discrimination of content

Directions

This exercise uses the same statements. This time, circle the
letter of the statement that is an accurate reflection of the *content* of
the speaker's statement, of what *underlies* the speaker's feelings. More
than one statement may be correct.

1. "These counseling sessions have really done me a great deal of
good. I enjoy my work more. I actually look forward to meeting
new people. My husband and I are talking more directly and seriously and decently to each other. There's just so much more freedom in my life!"

This person feels alive and excited,

a. because life has so much to offer her right now.

b. but she also knows that she has to be cautious.

c. because she knows that there will always be a counselor to help her.

d. because she's so much freer now—with herself, with others, and at
work.

e. because she's handling her depression well.

34

2. "My husband and I just decided to get a divorce. (*Pause*) I really don't look forward to the legal part of it—to *any* part of it. And, to tell you the truth, I just don't know what to expect. (*Pause*) I'm well into middle age. I don't think another marriage is possible. (*Pause*) I just don't know what to expect."

Right now this person is pretty depressed,

a. because she realizes that she has failed in her marriage.

b. because her husband has let her down so badly.

c. because her future is so uncertain and bleak.

d. because there are some rough times ahead and she's not sure how she is going to handle them.

e. but she can handle things with some help from the counselor and her friends.

f. but she realizes that we all go through trying times.

3. "My best friend has just turned her back on me. And I don't even know why. From the way she acted, I think she thinks I've been talking behind her back. Damn! This neighborhood is *full* of gossips. I hope she hasn't been listening to those foulmouths who just want to stir up trouble."

This person is really upset;

a. she doesn't want her friendship to be the victim of some malicious gossip.

b. it's frustrating to her because she's not sure what's really going on.

c. she's been loyal to her friend, but now the friend has let her down.

d. she'd really like to tell her friend and the whole neighborhood off.

e. she knows that *she* wouldn't act like that.

4. "My teacher told me today that I've done better work than she ever expected. I always thought that I could be good at studies if I really tried. So I risked it this semester, and it paid off."

So now this person feels competent and satisfied,

a. because he showed the teacher a thing or two.

b. because he did better than the others, and that's always a good feeling.

c. because this is just the beginning—he knows he's headed for the top.

d. because he's lived up to his *own* expectations.

e. because he put himself on the line and made things turn out well.

5. "I should never have allowed my daughter to go to the movies alone.
    I don't know what my wife will say when she gets home from work.
    She says I'm careless—but being careless with the kids—that's
    something else. I almost feel as if *I* had broken Karen's arm, not
    the guy in that car."

This person feels ashamed and miserable,

a. but he'll think positively and try to help his wife to do so also.

b. thinking of what might have happened to Karen—and he still has to
    face his wife.

c. but the worst is over.

d. and Karen's pain and his wife's anger will make him face his care-
    lessness.

e. but he's really learned a good lesson, and that's what counts.

6. "I've been in college two years now, and nothing much has happened.
    The teachers here are only so-so. And you can't say that the so-
    cial life around here is much. Things go on the same from day to
    day, week after week."

This person is bored,

a. because life around here doesn't seem to offer much.

b. because he really doesn't do much to make life interesting.

c. because neither school nor social life offers any challenge.

d. and he'd like to get out of here.

e. there doesn't seem much for him to invest himself in.

7. "I've finally met a woman who is very genuine and who lets me be
    myself. I can care about her deeply without making a child of her.
    And she cares about me without mothering me. It's a good, solid
    feeling. We've been thinking about getting married."

This person seems at peace and contented,

a. because he's been wanting to get married for a long time.

b. because there's mutual caring without overprotectiveness.

c. because there aren't many women like her around.

36

d. because here's an honest, nonpossessive relationship.

e. but he really hasn't known her long enough to be absolutely sure.

8. "Why does my husband keep blaming me for his trouble with the kids?
    I'm always in the middle. He complains to me about them. They
    complain to me about him. I could walk right out on the whole
    thing. Who the hell do they think they are?"

This person really resents

a. being in a damned-if-she-does, damned-if-she-doesn't situation.

b. being a go-between. Why don't they deal directly with one
    another?

c. being treated like the one who is to blame.

d. being in the middle—but she knows that she lets herself get caught
    there.

e. being practically forced out of her own house.

9. "I [a group trainee] don't know what to expect from this group.
    I've never been in a group before. I get the feeling that the rest
    of you are pros, so I'm afraid that I won't do what's right. I
    want to learn how to be a helper, but I'm not sure I can do that
    in this group."

This person feels uncomfortable and inadequate,

a. because she thinks that she has no talent.

b. because this is her first group experience and she doesn't know
    whether she's as talented as the other members.

c. but, still, she doesn't want to let herself down by leaving.

d. because she feels that she's the "low man on the totem pole."

e. but, actually, the others are just as scared as she is.

f. because it's very important for her to succeed.

10. "I [a client] don't know what I'm doing here. You're the third
    counselor they've sent me to—or is it the fourth? None of them
    did anything for me. In fact, I've never been interested. Why
    do they keep making me come here? It's a waste of your time and
    a waste of mine. Let's just fold the show right now."

This person feels that counseling is futile,

a. just like all the other times.

b. but maybe he'd like to try just once more.

c. because this is something *they* want him to do, not something he wants to do himself.

d. because he's just too damned independent to be helped by *anybody*!

e. because deep down he really hates himself.

Exercise 16: The active discrimination of feelings

Directions

Read the following statements; then write down a number of adjectives or phrases describing how the speaker feels.

1. Seventh-grade girl to teacher, outside class:
"My classmates don't like me, and right now I don't like them! Why do they have to be so mean? They make fun of me—well, at least they make fun of my clothes. My family can't afford to buy what those snots wear. Gee whiz, they don't have to like me, but I wish they'd stop making fun of me."

How does this person feel? _____

_____

2. Elderly woman in hospital with a broken hip:
"When you get old, you have to expect things like this to happen. I'm glad it wasn't any worse. Oh, I hate lying here like this, but let me tell you, there are a lot of people in here a lot worse off than I am. And there are more out in the world who are a lot worse off than all of us! I'm not a complainer. I never have been, and I'm not going to start now. I'm not saying that the people here give the best service—who does these days?—but it's a good thing these hospitals exist."

How does this person feel? _____

_____

3. Ghetto resident, 17, talking about the police:
"Who the hell do they think they are, pushing us around like that? They don't know anything. Everyone around here is just trash to them. Everyone's the same. You just look funny at them and you're guilty. And they think they can push you around. They don't live here. They're the strangers. They hate it here, and we end up paying for it."

How does this person feel? _____

_____

4. Businessman, 45, to his wife:
"I really don't know what my boss wants. I don't know how he feels about me. He says I'm doing fine, even when nothing special is happening, and I don't think I'm doing anything special. Then he blows up over nothing at all. He's so inconsistent. I don't know whether it's just that he's so erratic or that I don't know what's going on. It makes me begin to wonder about myself—whether I'm in the right job."

How does this person feel? _____

_____

5. Man, 55, talking with the trainer in a human-relations-training group:
"I'm a very private person. It takes me a long time to warm up to people and to open up. I certainly don't feel like revealing my secrets here. I don't think this is the place for it. I hope the others aren't going to be trying to make me "come clean" or parade my psyche around. That's just not me. Right now, I'm not sure what's going to happen."

How does this person feel? _____

_____

6. Girl, 19, to friend:
"Kevin, I really had a wonderful time with you today. I liked every minute of it. I had no idea that you could be so considerate or that you had such a sense of humor. To tell you the truth, I was afraid that you'd be stuffy or self-centered, or that you'd treat me like a 'good time.' I'm not sure where I picked up those ideas. Sometimes I'm a victim of my own prejudices."

How does this person feel? _____

_____

7. Woman, 39, in hospital dying of cancer, talking to chaplain:
"I can understand it from my children, but not from my husband. I know that I'm dying. But he comes here with that brave smile every day, hiding what *he* feels. We never talk about my dying. I know he's trying to protect me, but it's unreal. I actually keep feeling more and more distant from him every day. I can't tell him that his cheerfulness and his refusal to talk about my sickness is actually painful for me."

How does this person feel? _____

_____

8. High school counselor, 40, to a colleague:
    "Sometimes I think I'm living a lie. I have no real interest in
    high school kids. They actually bore me. So when they come into
    my office, I don't really do much to help them. But I've been here
    now for twelve years, and I'm settled in the community. I don't
    know whether I could really carry off a change. At times I've
    tried to work up more interest in this profession, but I can hardly
    say that I've succeeded."

How does this person feel? _____

_____

9. Trainee in a counselor-education program, talking to the trainer:
    "I'm beginning to see that my need to be a 'good guy' and to always
    be accepted by everyone makes me overeager with clients. But now
    that I've been able to identify what I'm doing, I've begun to
    change. When I take the part of the client in practice sessions, I
    talk about my need for approval. I'm beginning to see that I can do
    a good job as a helper without needing to be loved by everyone. I
    know I'm headed in the right direction."

How does this person feel? _____

_____

Exercise 17: The active discrimination of content

Directions

    Reread the client statements in the preceding exercise. Then com-
plete the following statements, indicating the reason or reasons underlying the feelings described.

1. She feels angry and humiliated *because* _____

_____

_____

2. She feels relatively at peace *because* _____

_____

_____

3. He feels enraged and fed up *because* _____

_____

_____

4. He feels on edge and uncertain *because* _____

_____

_____

5. He feels cautious and apprehensive *because* _____

_____

_____

6. She feels delighted *because* _____

_____

_____

7. She feels angry and hurt *because* _____

_____

_____

8. She feels guilty and caught in a bind *because* _____

_____

_____

9. He feels confident and pleased *because* _____

_____

_____

THE COMMUNICATION OF PRIMARY-LEVEL ACCURATE EMPATHY

The following exercises (18 to 24) deal with the communication of accurate empathy—that is, speaking *to* the client directly—rather than with the accurate identification of feelings and content. "Speaking out" your understanding in writing is one way of helping you to do so in actual face-to-face contact with a client.

Up to now, we have been using the third person—"he/she feels . . . because . . ."—in the exercises. Now we will switch to the second person—"you." In doing the following exercises, try to imagine your-self, as vividly as possible, actually listening to and talking to some-one. In the beginning, you will be asked to use the formulas "You feel . . ." and "You feel . . . because . . . ." Later on, you will be asked to translate these stylized formulas into more natural language—*your* language.

Exercise 18: The communication of the accurate understanding of one feeling

Directions

Imagine yourself listening to each of the people quoted below. Try to communicate to each person an accurate understanding of his or her feelings, using adjectives or phrases. Find a couple of adjectives and/ or phrases for each exercise.

1. Young woman, 23:
   "Jane and Sue showed up at the party in dresses *and* with dates. And there I was, alone and in slacks!"

You felt _____

2. Man, 65:
   "My wife died last year, and this year my youngest son went away to college. The other children are married. So now that I'm retired, I spend a lot of time rambling around a house that's really too big for me."

You feel _____

3. Married woman, 33:
   "I can't believe it! Tom came home on time for supper every day last week. I never thought he would live up to the contract we made."

You feel _____

4. Man, 40, talking about his invalid mother:
   "She uses her illness to control me. It's a pattern; she's been controlling me all her life. I bet she'll even make me feel re-sponsible for her death."

You feel _____

5. Young woman, 25, talking about her current boyfriend:
   "I can't quite figure him out. I still can't tell if he really cares about me, or if he's just trying to get me into bed."

You feel _____

6. Man, 35:
   "I'm going to the hospital tomorrow for some tests. The doctor
   suspects an ulcer. But nobody has told me exactly what kind of
   tests. I'm supposed to take these enemas and not eat anything
   tomorrow. I've heard rumors about what these tests are like,
   but I don't really know."

You feel _____

7. Woman, 28, talking about her job:
   "It's not a big thing. But this is the third time this month I've
   been asked to change hours with her. It certainly seems to indicate who is more important there. Why does it always have to be
   me who defers to her?"

You feel _____

8. Student, 16, talking about his teacher:
   "I thought he was going to really chew me out. I was afraid that
   he was just going to tell me he was kicking me out of class. But
   we sat in his office and talked about our differences!"

You feel _____

9. High school girl, 17, to male counselor:
   "I don't think I can talk about it here. What happens between me
   and my boyfriend and between me and my family is too personal.
   You're like a stranger to me, and I don't tell personal things to
   strangers."

You feel _____

10. Graduate student, 25, to adviser:
    "I have two term papers due tomorrow. I'm giving a report in class
    this afternoon. My wife is down with the flu. And now I find out
    that a special committee wants to 'talk' with me about my 'prog-
    ress' in the program."

You feel _____

11. Trainee in a counselor-education program, 21, to a fellow trainee:
    "I know he's going to ask me to counsel someone before the whole
    group. I can't even imagine myself standing up there! I actually
    feel like skipping the class and telling him I was sick."

You feel _____

Exercise 19: The communication of the accurate understanding of content (one emotion)

Directions

Reread the statements of Exercise 18. This time, focus on communicating accurate empathic understanding of the experiences and behaviors that give rise to the client's feelings.

1. You felt out of place *because* _____

_____

_____

2. You feel lonely *because* _____

_____

_____

3. You feel surprised *because* _____

_____

_____

4. You feel victimized *because* _____

_____

_____

5. You feel cautious *because* _____

_____

_____

6. You feel apprehensive *because* _____

_____

_____

7. You feel irritated *because* _____

_____

_____

8. You feel pleasantly surprised *because* _____

_____

_____

9. You feel reluctant to talk about your problems *because* —————

——————————————————————————————

——————————————————————————————

10. You feel overwhelmed *because* ——————————————

——————————————————————————————

——————————————————————————————

11. You feel panic *because* ————————————————

——————————————————————————————

——————————————————————————————

Exercise 20: The communication of the accurate understanding of more than one feeling

Directions

    In the following statements, the speaker expresses more than one feeling or emotion. In your response, communicate your understanding of the speaker's feelings or emotions. For the present, please use the formula, "You feel both . . . and . . . ."

1. Factory worker, 30:
    "Work is okay. I do make a good living, and my family really likes the money. And they like me at work; they like what I do, so my job is secure. But it's the same thing day after day. I'm not the world's brightest person, but there's more to me than I use working on those machines."

You feel both ————————————————————

——————————————————————————————

2. Mental-hospital inpatient, 54:
    "To tell you the truth, I *like it here*. So I don't see why everybody in this group is so eager to get me out. Who says I can't like it here? Who says I shouldn't like it here? Is that a crime? I know you're all interested in me. That's what keeps me coming to these sessions. But do I have to prove that I care about you by leaving this place?"

You feel both ————————————————————

——————————————————————————————

45

3. Outpatient, 60, at local community mental-health center:
   "I've never asked anyone for help in my life—never needed to. And here I am, at your doorstep, week after week. What's happened to me? Where has my manhood gone? Damn it! Nothing has licked me yet, and I'm not going to let depression get the best of me."

You feel both _____

_____

4. Juvenile-probation officer to colleague:
   "These kids really drive me up the wall. Sometimes I think I'm really stupid to be doing this kind of work. They taunt me. They push me as far as they can. To some of them, I'm just another 'pig.' But every time I think of quitting—damn it—I know I'd miss this kind of work and even—one way or another—miss the kids. When I wake up in the morning, I know the day's going to be full and it's going to demand everything I've got."

You feel both _____

_____

5. Teacher, 50, to a colleague:
   "Cindy Smith really got to me today. She's been a thorn in my side all semester. Just a little bitch. Asking questions in her 'sweet' way, but everyone knows she's trying to make an ass of me. Little snot! So I let her have it—I pasted her up against the wall verbally. You know me: I ordinarily don't do that kind of thing. I lost control. It was awful. I have no love for Cindy, but it was a pretty bad mistake."

You feel both _____

_____

6. Mother, talking about her 17-year-old son:
   "He knows he can take advantage of me. If he stops talking to me or acts sullen for a couple of days, I go crazy. He gets everything he wants out of me, and I know it's my own fault. I don't even think of trying to stop him. I need him very much."

You feel both _____

_____

7. Minister, 45, at a career-counseling center:
   "To tell the truth, I think the synod administration has really mistreated me. I put my name in last year for a change in parishes, and I haven't heard a thing. I know I've been passed over, but they haven't even had the courtesy to talk to me about it. How can we expect to minister to congregations when we can't even minister to one another? I know what my talents are, I know what I

46

can do. I *do* have talents I can use to help people, and I *don't*
have to do it in the ministry. I'm going to start looking around
for a job in some other helping profession."

You feel both _____

_____

8. Secretary, 35:
"I've been a garden-variety secretary for over three years now.
But last week the boss's personal secretary died suddenly, and he
chose *me* to take her place. I never expected that. More money,
everything! Now I'm not so sure I can fill her shoes. She was *so*
competent. And he left so many things in her hands."

You feel both _____

_____

9. Woman, 35, at a mental-health center:
"My greatest asset and my greatest cross to bear is my husband. He
loves me, he shows me all sorts of consideration and affection. I
can't help but love him. But he's a terrible liar. He goes around
the neighborhood telling tall tales. This started about a year ago.
It's getting so bad that I don't dare appear in public."

You feel both _____

_____

10. Office worker, 59:
"I don't know if it's just me. The last few years, we've hired a
lot of young people and a lot of minority people in the office.
Now it doesn't seem like the same place. It's not a family.
They're all polite to me, but that's about it. I've tried making
new friends, but I don't seem to be 'with it' enough. I'm not sure
that I want to try anymore, or that it's even worth it."

You feel both _____

_____

*Exercise 21: The communication of the accurate understanding of content
(more than one emotion)*

Directions

Once you have checked the accuracy of your understanding of the
speaker's emotions, check your understanding of the *content* of his
statement. Still using the formula "You feel . . . because . . . ,

47

write out a complete statement of accurate empathy for the statements in Exercise 20. Number 1 is an example.

1. <u>You feel both satisfied and dissatisfied because, although your job has many material advantages, it still doesn't satisfy *you* or use your best resources.</u>

2.

3.

4.

5.

6.

7.

8. _____

_____

_____

_____

9. _____

_____

_____

_____

10. _____

_____

_____

_____

Exercise 22: The communication of primary-level accurate empathy: Feeling and content (one emotion)

Directions

Read the following statements. Try to imagine that the person is speaking directly to you. Respond with primary-level accurate empathy.

a. Respond first by using the formula "You feel . . . because . . . ."
b. Then write a response that includes understanding of both feelings and content but that is cast in your own language and style. Make this second response as natural as possible.

Number 1 is an example.

1. Law student to school counselor:
"I learned yesterday that I've flunked out of school and that there's no recourse. I've seen everybody, but the door is shut tight. What a mess! I have no idea how I'll face my parents. They've paid for my college education and this year of law school. And now I'll have to tell them that it's all down the drain."

a. "You must feel awful—helpless, because you've been dropped from school, and ashamed, because you've let your parents down."

_____

b. "Your world has come crashing down. It's really painful to be dropped from school, but maybe it's even more painful to face your parents with the fact, after all they've done for you."

2. College teacher to a colleague:
"I should have my head examined. I've really been dumb. To make a long story short, I've let myself fall in love with one of the girls in my class. You know—the classic story. She was so friendly, and I thought it wouldn't hurt to be a little friendly in return. And now my emotions are all screwed up. And so are hers."

a. _____

_____

_____

_____

b. _____

_____

_____

_____

3. College student to a counselor:
"Last year I was drinking heavily and playing around with drugs. I had to drop three courses and almost ended up on probation. And today, it's practically the opposite. I woke up in my own vomit one morning and said 'God, this can't go on—I'm killing myself.' Nobody lectured me, nobody pushed me. I began making the right kind of friends. And I pulled myself up out of the muck."

a. _____

_____

_____

_____

b. _____

_____

4. Sailor, 18, to a chaplain:
   "I just can't go on that ship. You've got to get me off. I get
   all the dirty work around here. And now we're going on a seven-
   month cruise. I'm just going to be a slave out there. Seven
   months! I'll go out of my mind. You've just got to get me off."

a. _____

   _____

   _____

   _____

b. _____

   _____

   _____

   _____

5. Postoperative patient, 40, to a nurse:
   "Can't you people do anything more for this pain? One injection
   every four hours doesn't even make a dent in it. You've been
   solving the problem by ignoring me. Nobody comes in here when I
   push that damn button. What kind of place is this, anyway?"

a. _____

   _____

   _____

   _____

b. _____

   _____

   _____

   _____

6. Young man, 21, to a job counselor:
   "Sure I'm only 21 and divorced already! I made a stupid mistake.
   I was a dumb, impulsive, self-centered kid at 18. The 'marriage'
   was a farce—a chance to get into bed without our parents' scream-
   ing at us. But is something I did at 18 going to count against me
   for the rest of my life?"

a. _____

_____

_____

_____

b. _____

_____

_____

_____

7. Counselor trainee in a group of his fellow trainees, addressing one
    trainee in particular:
    "You always rate me low—lower than anyone else here. I don't
    think you like me, and I don't think you've been honest enough to
    deal with it out in the open. That's just how I feel right now."

a. _____

_____

_____

_____

b. _____

_____

_____

_____

8. PTA member to a friend:
    "I got up there, and nothing would come out. I couldn't even re-
    member the topic of my talk. Nothing like that has ever happened
    to me before. I couldn't even say that nothing would come out! So
    I just sat down."

a. _____

_____

_____

_____

b. _____

_____

52

9. College senior to school counselor:
   "I want to go to medical school more than anything else in the
   world. I'd also like to get married, but my mother says that once
   I marry, I'll be completely on my own. She's footing the bill for
   my education. I don't have a red cent."

a. _____

   _____

   _____

b. _____

   _____

   _____

10. Client, 43, to counselor:
    "Your suggestion that we take a look at my strengths and resources
    hits me between the eyes. You know, I don't think I've ever done
    that in my whole life. What a waste. I've just moped along think-
    ing I was nothing."

a. _____

   _____

   _____

b. _____

   _____

   _____

Directions

In the following statements, the client expresses at least two distinct emotional states. Respond with primary-level accurate empathy.

a. First, use the formal "You feel . . . because . . . ."
b. Then respond using your own language and style, dealing with both emotional states.

Number 1 is an example.

1. Woman, 48, to counselor:
"It's been a long haul. The operation left me with only one lung, so I'll never be as active as I used to be. But at least I'm beginning to see that life is still worth living. I have to take a long look at the possibilities, no matter how much they've narrowed. There's something stirring inside me—that old person who doesn't want to give up."

a. Even though you feel cautious because you're no longer 100% well

physically, you're hopeful that life still has much to offer.

_____

b. It sounds as if the sun is beginning to break through after a long

winter. You're cautious but determined to make it. There *are*

possibilities.

2. Woman, 41, to counselor:
"To put it frankly, I don't think my husband is interested in me sexually anymore. We haven't slept together for over two months. I never let myself think that this could happen to me. Now it's practically all I think of. I thought I could handle it, but I lie awake at night or pace up and down. What should I do?"

a. _____

_____

_____

_____

b. _____

_____

_____

_____

3. Man, 57, to counselor:
"My younger brother—he's 53—has always been kind of a bum. He's always poaching off the rest of the family. The last couple of years, it's been getting worse; he's been showing up and asking for 'loans.' Last week my sister told me that she'd been foolish enough to give him some money for a 'business deal.' Business deal, my foot! I'd like to get ahold of him and kick his ass. Oh, he's not a vicious guy. Just weak. He's never been able to grab hold of life. It's enough to make you weep. But he's got the whole family in a turmoil now, and we can't keep going through hell for him."

a. _____

_____

_____

_____

b. _____

_____

_____

_____

4. Man, 33, to counselor:
"Actually, it's a relief to tell someone. I don't have to give you any excuses or make the story sound right. I drink because I like to drink; I'm just crazy about the juice, that's all. But telling you is not going to get me anywhere. When I get out of here, I know I'm going to go straight to a bar and drink."

a. _____

_____

_____

_____

b. _____

_____

_____

_____

5. Woman, 43, talking about her friend to counselor:
   "I know I caused her some sleepless nights by talking about her
   behind her back. I should have known that it couldn't be kept
   quiet. I thought it shouldn't have been kept quiet. I was wrong.
   But she won't let me be open with her. She's so sensitive. I
   have to watch what I say and how I say it when I'm with her. Unless we can talk openly with each other, I'm not sure I can be her
   friend."

a. _____

_____

_____

_____

b. _____

_____

_____

_____

6. High school senior to school counselor:
   "My dad told me the other night that I looked relaxed. Well, I
   don't feel relaxed. I'm not going out of my mind right now, because we're between semesters, but next semester I'm signed up for
   two math courses, and math really rips me up. But I'll need it for
   the science, since I want to go into pre-med."

a. _____

_____

_____

_____

b. _____

_____

_____

_____

*Exercise 24: The practice of primary-level accurate empathy in everyday
life*

   If the communication of accurate empathy is to become part of your
natural communication style, you will have to practice it outside of the

formal training sessions. If accurate empathy is relegated exclusively
to officially designated helping sessions, it may never prove genuine.
Actually, practicing accurate empathy is a relatively simple process.

1. Begin to observe conversations between people from the viewpoint
    of the communication of accurate empathic understanding. Does a
    person generally take the time to communicate to another person
    this kind of understanding? Try to discover whether, in everyday
    life, the communication of accurate empathic understanding
    (primary-level) is frequent or rare. As you listen to conversa-
    tions, keep a behavioral count of these interactions (without
    changing your own interpersonal style or interfering with the con-
    versation of others).
2. Try to observe how often you use the communication of accurate
    empathic understanding as part of your communication style. In the
    beginning, don't try to increase the number of times you use accu-
    rate empathy in day-to-day conversations. Merely observe your
    usual behavior.
3. Increase the number of times you use accurate empathy in day-to-day
    conversations. Again, without being phony or overly preoccupied
    with the project, try to keep some kind of behavioral count. Don't
    make a fetish of accurate empathy. Use it more frequently, but do
    so genuinely. You will soon discover that there are a great number
    of opportunities for using accurate empathy genuinely.
4. Observe the impact your use of primary-level accurate empathy has
    upon others. Don't *use* others for your own experimentation, but,
    once you increase your use of genuine accurate empathy, try to see
    what it does for the communication process.

SECTION 5
GENUINENESS AND RESPECT: A BEHAVIORAL PERSPECTIVE

Exercise 25: A checklist on the communication of genuineness

It is impossible to "practice" genuineness in and by itself. Genuineness refers to a set of attitudes and behaviors communicated by the helper to the client during the helping/communication process. However, although genuineness cannot be practiced separately, trainees can give one another feedback on the quality of genuineness they communicate during training sessions. In order to give *concrete* feedback, the trainees should have clearly in mind the behaviors that constitute the communication of genuineness. During Stage I, use the following criteria in giving one another feedback.

1. Is the helper (communicator) his natural self? Does he avoid projecting a stylized role of "counselor" that is overtly and overly "professional"? Does he avoid using professional jargon ("counselorese")?
2. Is the helper spontaneous (and yet tactful), or is there something rigid and planned about his behavior? Does he move easily with the client?
3. Does the helper avoid defensiveness, even when the client questions, challenges, or attacks him?
4. Does the helper express what he thinks and feels, with proper timing and without disturbing or distracting the client, but without putting a number of "filters" between himself and the client?
5. Is the helper open? Does he project a willingness to share himself (even though actual self-disclosure on his part might not yet be called for)?

Use this checklist as a matter of course in the beginning of the training process. Later on, use the checklist when it is required.

Exercise 26: A checklist on the communication of respect

It is impossible to "practice" respect in and by itself. Respect refers to a set of attitudes communicated to the client and to behaviors embedded in the communication process. However, although respect cannot be practiced separately, trainees can give one another feedback on whether the "helper" (communicator) is manifesting respect for the "client." Respect is also important in the process of giving feedback on helping and communication styles. In order to give *concrete* feedback, trainees should have clearly in mind the behaviors that constitute the communication of respect. During Stage I, use the following criteria in giving one another feedback on the communication of respect.

1. Does the helper (communicator) seem to be "for" the other in a nonsentimental, caring way?
2. Is the helper obviously *working* at communicating with the other?
3. Is the helper dealing with the other as a unique individual and not just as a "case"?
4. Does the helper avoid being judgmental?
5. Does the helper use accurate empathy frequently and effectively?
6. Does the helper communicate understanding of whatever *resources* the other reveals and not just understanding of his problems?
7. Is the helper appropriately warm? Does he avoid—equally—coldness, the intimate type of warmth that characterizes friendship, and the "canned" warmth of the counselor role?
8. Does the helper attend effectively?
9. Does the helper avoid statements or behaviors that might indicate a desire to exploit the other?
10. Does the helper find ways of reinforcing the other for what he does well (such as engage in painful self-exploration)?

Use whichever of these criteria are appropriate in giving feedback to your fellow trainees. Feedback on the communication of respect should take place early in the training process. Later on, it should be given only as required (for example, if a trainee shows some signs of exploiting his "client" in some way).

SECTION 6
PUTTING IT ALL TOGETHER IN STAGE I

Exercise 27: The identification of common mistakes in Stage I

The following exercise deals with some of the common mistakes that are made in responding to a client during Stage I. These faults or mistakes consist, in effect, of poor execution of primary-level accurate empathy. Before you do the exercise itself, let's review briefly what some of these common mistakes are.

   responses that imply condescension or manipulation
   premature advice or premature discussion of action programs
   premature use of advanced-level accurate empathy
   responses that indicate rejection of or lack of respect for the client
   responses involving premature confrontation
   responses that are patronizing or placating ("That's all right, now, everything will be all right")
   use of inaccurate primary-level empathy
   use of clichés
   incomplete or inadequate responses (saying "uh-huh" when primary-level accurate empathy is called for)
   responses that ignore the problem (responses that would change the subject or be otherwise irrelevant)
   use of questions that are closed, irrelevant, or inappropriate to Stage I
   use of inappropriate warmth or sympathy
   judgmental remarks
   premature use of immediacy
   premature, irrelevant, or otherwise inappropriate use of helper self-disclosure

This list is certainly not exhaustive. Can you think of other mistakes? Some of these errors are demonstrated in the exercise that follows. You are asked to identify them.
   However important it is to understand a person from his own frame of reference first, there is still a tendency *not* to do so—to do many other things instead. Below are a number of client statements followed by a number of possible responses.

60

Directions

First, if the response is good—that is, if it is primary-level accurate empathy—give it a plus sign; if it is an inadequate or poor response, give it a minus sign.

Second, for any response you rate with a minus sign, indicate the reason or reasons why it is a poor or inadequate response (for example, it shows disrespect; it is premature confrontation; it is premature advice). Make your reasons as specific as possible. One function of this exercise is to make us aware of the many different ways we can fail to communicate understanding in our interactions with others.

Example

Boy, 15, to school counselor:
"Mr. Jones has it in for me. We haven't gotten along from the start. I don't do anything different from the other guys, but when there's a blowup, I'm the first one to blame. I wish he'd get off my back."

Rating

a. (-) You ought to cool it in his class. Why get thrown out of there for something so stupid?

Reason: <u>premature advice</u>

b. (+) You feel he's being unfair to you—and that's lousy.

Reason: <u>(none because it is a plus)</u>

c. (-) You've been in trouble before. Are you really giving it to me straight?

Reason: <u>judgmental</u>

d. (-) Okay, Tom. We can straighten this whole thing out if we all just stay cool. I think we're all reasonable people. By the way, how's the family?

Reason: <u>placating; inappropriate, nonhelpful warmth</u>

1. Hospital patient, 58, to chaplain:
"They've been taking tests for three days now. I don't know what's going on. They don't tell me what they're for or what they find. The doctor comes in for a moment every now and then, but he doesn't tell me anything, either. And I still feel so weak and listless."

a. (   ) Well, these things take time, you know. This happens all the time.

Reason: _____

b. ( ) Is this the first time you've been in the hospital?

Reason: _____

c. ( ) Have your nurse call the doctor and just ask him what's going on.

Reason: _____

d. ( ) Well, now, perhaps a little more patience would help every-one, including you.

Reason: _____

2. Girl, 22, to job counselor:
"I wince every time people ask me about my education. As soon as I say 'high school,' I see their minds turn off. I feel that I'm as educated as any college grad. I read quite a bit. I deal with people well. I think I've got whatever you're supposed to get from college—except the degree. College isn't the only educator. I know some people who I think were retarded by college.

a. ( ) Uh-huh.

Reason: _____

b. ( ) You feel good because you've been the principal agent in your own education.

Reason: _____

c. ( ) You're not angry only at potential employers. You resent the whole system, and you'd like to show people a thing or two.

Reason: _____

d. ( ) You resent being categorized when you say 'high school.' You know you're an educated person.

Reason: _____

3. Man, 32, to counselor:
"I just *can't* divorce her. My parents would have kittens. They don't really like her, but they believe marriage is forever. They're Catholic, and my mother is especially devout. She follows all the rules. I don't go to church anymore, myself. But my parents aren't aware of that."

a. ( ) Is your wife Catholic?

Reason: _____

b. ( ) Maybe it's time to cut the apron strings. Your mother doesn't have to live with your wife. *You* do.

Reason: ───

c. ( ) You feel caught. You don't think your parents could really handle it if you divorced your wife.

Reason: ───

d. ( ) I got a divorce, and my parents finally learned how to live with it, even though they didn't like it.

Reason: ───

4. Deputy sheriff to a jail inspector:
"I feel like an errand boy around here rather than a law-enforcement officer. I get the prisoners cigarettes and coffee. It's the only way I can keep them from tearing up the place or tearing into one another. This place is unfit for humans. It's unfit for me, and I'm not even in a cell. There's nothing for them to do around here. We don't have space, we don't have programs."

a. ( ) Why don't you stop your complaining!

Reason: ───

b. ( ) You feel sorry for these guys, since often it's not their fault they're in here.

Reason: ───

c. ( ) I feel you have it in for me. You attack me because you can't get at the system. So you make *me* feel lousy.

Reason: ───

d. ( ) I saw your wife and kids at church the other day. They really look great.

Reason: ───

5. High school senior to teacher:
"I graduate at the end of the first semester. Then I could go right downstate to school. That has some advantages, like getting away from home sooner than I'd planned. And also getting a head start in college. But it also means leaving my friends here. And all the freshmen at the University are probably set up with their own friends in cliques by now. Maybe I should stick around and just enjoy doing nothing for a semester."

a. ( ) It's hard to decide. It would be kind of exciting to get away from home and start college. But you'd hate to end up without any friends.

Reason: ───

63

b. (   ) It seems that you really fear loneliness in your life.

Reason: _____

c. (   ) All of us have to face these decisions. But they give us character.

Reason: _____

d. (   ) When I was your age, I didn't have the luxury of having that kind of decision to make.

Reason: _____

6. Middle-level manager to organizational-development consultant:
   "These damn fools here don't know what they're doing. We're going to end up like the railroads. The union leaders keep pulling the noose tighter and tighter. If a guy even looks at a machine for which he isn't 'licensed,' there's an uproar. With the economy the way it is, there just has to be more leeway to move people around. But if you think you can talk some sense into these guys, you've got another think coming."

a. (   ) I'd like to have you elaborate on that a little more.

Reason: _____

b. (   ) I feel that if we all keep our heads, things can work out.
         You strike me as a sincere person. Let see if we can find some way of settling things down.

Reason: _____

c. (   ) You'd better come back here when you feel you can speak a bit more civilly.

Reason: _____

d. (   ) I feel you're attacking *me*, even though I'm not part of the problem. Maybe we can talk out what's happening between you and me.

Reason: _____

7. Woman, 54, to clergyman:
   "Nothing's been right since my husband died, two years ago. I literally slave for these children. Up early to get to work. Back in the evening to get meals. Housekeeping on the weekends. You'd think those kids would have more gratitude and help me a little. But the older they get, the more selfish they get."

a. ( ) You deserve better than this, Mary. I *know* what kind of worker you are. You shouldn't have to work as hard as you do—day and night.

Reason: ───────────────────────────────────

b. ( ) Mary, the gospel says that if they force you to go one mile, go two miles with them. It doesn't sound like you're ready to go that second mile.

Reason: ───────────────────────────────────

c. ( ) You have to be a better disciplinarian. Take away their privileges if they don't shape up. You're headed for an early grave.

Reason: ───────────────────────────────────

d. ( ) It's really unfair, then. You feel that they should all pitch in and do their part.

Reason: ───────────────────────────────────

8. Resident of a halfway house, 58, to a caseworker:
"You always hang around with the younger residents, playing pool and ping pong and listening to that awful music. I have to sit in the dining room alone. When you do talk to me, I get the feeling you think you're wasting your time."

a. ( ) You're just jealous of the younger people.

Reason: ───────────────────────────────────

b. ( ) Come sit with me now and we'll work everything out. We can have a nice chat.

Reason: ───────────────────────────────────

c. ( ) I really don't like the young people at all. I have to force myself to be with them.

Reason: ───────────────────────────────────

d. ( ) Do you think that the other caseworkers deal with you like this?

Reason: ───────────────────────────────────

9. Mental-health center inpatient, 24, to aide:
"Do you know what happened last night? I went to see that stupid

psychiatrist who comes around here. And all he did was spend ten minutes with me, and he didn't say anything. I bet he makes a bundle for doing nothing. You know, he never really spends time with anybody."

a. (　) Trying to deal with authority figures tends to pull you apart.

Reason: ───

b. (　) Talk to me about something else. I've heard this record before.

Reason: ───

c. (　) I can see that you're scared by that kind of treatment.

Reason: ───

d. (　) You feel he doesn't give you enough time, and you're irritated.

Reason: ───

10. Mental-hospital inpatient, 37, to nurse, during passing of medication:
"I haven't taken my meds in a week, and I feel great. I don't need a doctor to tell me what's good for me. And I don't need you to try to get me to take that junk."

a. (　) Everybody gets mad about his medicine now and then.

Reason: ───

b. (　) If you help us by taking your medicine, then we can help you.

Reason: ───

c. (　) Who gives a damn whether you take it or not?

Reason: ───

d. (　) I'm a daughter-figure for you, and you know you can't deal with that.

Reason: ───

Exercise 28: Counseling oneself: An exercise in Stage-I skills

In this exercise, you are asked to carry on a dialogue with yourself.
Choose a problematic area in your life. Try to choose one that is relevant to your interpersonal style and/or to your competence as a

helper. Use the skills of Stage I to help yourself explore this problem. Stay in Stage I; don't confront yourself or start elaborating action programs for yourself.

First, study the following example.

Example

This example deals with a beginning counselor trainee who has been working for a while in a halfway house for people who have been in mental hospitals.

Self: I'm not so sure I should be working at that halfway house. I've studied a lot of psychology in the last three years of college, but it hasn't been the kind of stuff that helps me with my job. I'm not sure whether I'm helping anybody there or not. I'm a willing worker, but I'm not sure how effective I am.

Response to self: You just don't feel prepared to do what you're doing. You work hard, but you still feel inadequate.

Self: Yeah. I'm pretty much on my own there. I have to figure out what to do. In a sense, I'm trusted; but, since I don't get much supervision, I have to go on my own instincts, and I'm not sure they're always right.

Response: Being left to your own devices doesn't increase your sense of personal adequacy. There's still that what-am-I-doing-here feeling.

Self: Sure! There are days when I ask myself just that: what am I doing here? I provide day-to-day services for a lot of people. I listen to them. I take them to the doctor. I try to help them participate with one another in conversation and games and things like that. I try to urge them to be responsible for their personal appearance and for the house. But it seems that I'm always just meeting the needs of the moment. I don't feel that I'm helping these people reach any long-range goals.

Response: You don't feel that there's a great deal of substance or much overall direction to what you're doing, and that's depressing.

Self: I *am* depressed. I'm down on myself. Down on the house and the directors. I feel that the most honest thing to do is to quit.

Response: Saying good-by to the job seems to fit in best with your emotional state right now.

SECTION 7
THE SKILLS OF STAGE II

ADVANCED ACCURATE EMPATHY

Clients, if they are to understand themselves and their problems in a way that enables them to see the need for action and behavioral change, must be helped to get a more objective frame of reference than the one from which they have been viewing their problems. Advanced accurate empathy helps them do this.

Advanced accurate empathy can be expressed in a number of ways. These are reviewed briefly below. Before doing the following exercises, however, review the sections on advanced accurate empathy in *The Skilled Helper*.

Try to help the client see the "bigger picture." ("The problem doesn't seem to be just your brother-in-law; your resentment seems to spread somewhat to his fellow workers.")

Help the client see what he expresses indirectly or implies but does not express directly. ("I think I might also be hearing you say that you are more than disappointed—perhaps even somewhat angry.")

Help the client see some of the logical conclusions of what he is saying. ("Do I hear you saying that, since you have lost all enthusiasm for school, you'd like to drop out, at least for a while?")

Help the client open up areas at which he only hints. ("You've brought up sexual matters a number of times. My guess is that sex is a pretty touchy issue with you—but pretty important, too.")

Help the client see what he may be overlooking. ("I wonder if it's possible that some people take your wit too personally, that they see it as sarcasm rather than humor.")

Help the client identify themes. ("You've mentioned several times, in different ways, that people you don't know make you uncomfortable and even frighten you. Is that the way you see it?")

Help the client own his only partially owned feelings and behaviors. ("I'm not sure whether or not you are saying that you actually do want to court her.")

Tentativeness is important at this stage in the helping process. Always include some indication of tentativeness when expressing advanced accurate empathy to the client so that the client will not take your understanding as an accusation.

In the preceding examples, point out the words that indicate that the responses are tentative. Enumerate other ways in which tentativeness can be expressed.

Exercise 29: The distinction between primary-level and advanced accurate empathy

In the following exercise, assume that the helper and the client have established rapport and that the client is beginning to explore his feelings, experiences, and behavior rather freely. Some flavor of this rapport will be given under the heading "context."

Directions

1. Review the sections in *The Skilled Helper* dealing with advanced accurate empathy.
2. Imagine the client speaking directly to you, and then do two things:

   a. First, respond with primary-level accurate empathy.
   b. Then respond with some statement of advanced accurate empathy. Try to help the client take the larger view of his problem, see the implications or logical conclusions of what he is saying, and so on.

Example

Father of family, 48, to counselor:

Context: This man is exploring the poor relationships he has with his wife and children. In general, he feels that *he* is the victim, that his family is not treating him right. He has not yet started to examine the implications of his own behavior.

"I get a lot of encouragement for being witty at parties. Almost everybody laughs—and heartily. I think that I provide a lot of entertainment, and that others like it. But this is another way I flop at home. When I try to be funny, my wife and kids don't laugh. At times, they take the whole thing wrong and get angry. I actually have to watch myself in my own home."

a. *primary-level accurate empathy*: "What you see as good entertainment just doesn't go over at home. And your failure mystifies and maybe even irritates you."

b. *advanced accurate empathy*: "You get irritated when your family responds to you so differently. It almost sounds as if they don't

69

want to see you as an entertainer at home. I wonder if perhaps they would simply prefer to have a straightforward you."

1. First-year engineering graduate student to counselor:

Context: This student has been exploring his disappointment with himself and with his performance in graduate school. He has explored such issues as his dislike for the school and for some of the teachers.

"I just don't have much enthusiasm. My grades are just okay—maybe even a little below par. I know I could do better if I wanted to. I don't know why my disappointment in the school and in some of the faculty members can get to me so much. Ever since I can remember—even in grammar school, when I didn't have any idea what an engineer was—I've wanted to be an engineer. Theoretically, I should be happy as a lark. Or at least I shouldn't be this depressed."

a. _____
_____
_____
_____

b. _____
_____
_____
_____

2. Man, 66, to counselor:

Context: This man has retired. He has been exploring with the counselor some of the problems his retirement has created.

"The kids are all gone. My wife died two years ago. And now that I've stopped working, I seem just to ramble around the house aimlessly—which is not like me at all. I suppose I should get rid of the house, but it's filled with lots of memories—bittersweet memories, now. There were a lot of good years here. The years seem to have slipped by and caught me unaware."

a. _____
_____
_____
_____

b. _____

_____

_____

_____

3. Woman, 33, to clergyman:

Context: This woman has been examining the quality of her interpersonal life. She is not married. She has one very close friend whom she counts on a great deal. She has been exploring her general interpersonal style and, specifically, her relationship with this one close friend.

"Ruth and I are on and off like electric lights with each other lately. When we're on, it's great. We have lunch together often enough, go shopping—you know, all that kind of stuff. The companionship is great. But sometimes she seems to just click off. She's been off for two weeks now. I can tell it in her voice on the phone. Why do we always have to have these falling-outs? I know we're different types. She's rather quiet, and I'm loud—the blasting type. But our differences don't ordinarily get in our way. At least I don't think so."

a. _____

_____

_____

_____

b. _____

_____

_____

_____

4. Man, 40, to marriage counselor:

Context: This is the third time that this man has come to see a marriage counselor during the past four years. His wife has never come with him. He spends only a session or two with the counselor and then drops out.

"I could go on telling you what she does and doesn't do. It's a litany. She really knows how to punish. I don't see how I've put up with it this long. I keep telling her to see a counselor. She won't do it. So here I am again, in her place. I've told this story over and over again, but it doesn't help. I've tried almost everything."

71

a. _____

_____

_____

_____

b. _____

_____

_____

_____

5. High school senior to school counselor:

Context: This girl expected that she would be chosen valedictorian of her class. Her parents counted on it; she counted on it. She's trying to deal with her disappointment.

"I know that I would have liked to be the class valedictorian—I mean, insofar as that's something that can be desired. They chose Jane. She's a good person, and she'll do a good job. She speaks well. She's popular. And, after all, no one has a *right* to be valedictorian. I'd be kidding myself if I thought differently. I've done better in school than Jane, but I'm not as popular. It's certainly nothing I can get angry over."

a. _____

_____

_____

_____

b. _____

_____

_____

_____

6. College professor, 43, to a friend who is a counselor:

Context: He is interested in examining his hierarchy of values. He is vaguely dissatisfied with it, and he talks to his friends about it from time to time. He has just come from a depressing day of classes.

"I'm depressed. I don't feel like working any more today. I actually work all the time. I can't think of any day I get up that I don't intend to devote to work. I think I even begrudge myself the time I take for relaxation. There's been no day in the past couple of years when I've said 'Well, today's a day off. I'll go out and do what I want.' I thought that all that I wanted to do was work. After all, it's my choice! I do what I do freely."

a. _____

_____

_____

_____

b. _____

_____

_____

_____

7. Man, 54, to counselor:

Context: This man has a variety of problems. His tendency is to ruminate constantly on his defects.

"To feel bad, all I have to do is review what has happened in my life and take a good look at what's going on now. This past year, I let my drinking problem get the best of me for four months. Over the years, I've messed up my marriage. Now my wife and I are separated. I don't have the kind of job that can support two households, and the job market is really tight. I'm not so sure what skills I have to market, anyhow. I may be looking at the negative side of my life, but there's a hell of a lot of it."

a. _____

_____

_____

_____

b. _____

_____

_____

_____

8. Woman, 35, to counselor:

Context: This woman is divorced. She has a daughter about 12 years old. She has been talking about her current relationships with men, reporting

that she has lied to her daughter about the sexual aspects of these relationships.

"I don't want to hurt my daughter by letting her see my other side. I
don't know whether she could handle it. What do you think? I'd like
to tell her everything. I just don't want her to think less of me. I
like sex. I've been used to it in marriage, and it's just too hard to
give it up. I wish you'd give me an answer on what to do about my
daughter."

a. _____

_____

_____

_____

b. _____

_____

_____

_____

9. Woman, 32, talking to a friend.

Context: This woman has attended a play with a good friend. As they
leave the theater, she begins to ruminate on her life, as she has on a
number of other occasions.

"When I come out of a play like this, or a good movie, my spirits soar.
By tomorrow, I'll be back on the ground again. But there is something
good in letting my spirits soar from time to time. I hate intellectual
analyses of the 'meaning' of a movie or play. I just let myself flow
with its mood for a while, and the world seems bright and full of possibilities again. Tomorrow isn't here yet."

a. _____

_____

_____

_____

b. _____

_____

_____

_____

10. Man, 31, to his fellow group members:

Context: This man meets with this group once a week for a couple of hours. The members use the group experience to examine their life-styles, values, ways of inter-relating, family life, and so on. They know one another well. He has mentioned his mother on a few occasions before this session.

"My mother and I get along well. Oh, there are always those little mis-understandings with me or with my wife when she spends a few days at our house. But I'm sure this happens in most households. Mom is very self-reliant, and I admire her for that. She's strong-willed, and I think that's great in a woman her age. She won't buckle under to life. I had to calm my wife down just the other day after one of the little misun-derstandings. But we have to expect these.

a. _____

_____

_____

_____

b. _____

_____

_____

_____

Exercise 30: Summarizing as advanced accurate empathy

Directions

1. The training group is divided into triads: helper, helpee, and observer.
2. The helper spends ten minutes counseling the helpee, using primary-level accurate empathy. As usual, the helpee should deal with a problem area relevant to his interpersonal and/or helping style.
3. At the end of the ten minutes, the helper summarizes the principal points of the interaction. The summary should be both accurate and concise. Then the helper should add a statement of advanced accu-rate empathy (such as a statement spelling out the implications of the summary).
4. The helper and helpee then continue the interaction for two or three more interchanges in order to get a feeling for the helpful-ness of the summary and the advanced accurate empathy.
5. The helper receives feedback, from both the observer and the helpee, on the accuracy of his summary and the helpfulness of his advanced accurate empathy.

6. The triad should exchange roles until each person in the group has been the helper.

Example

Obviously, it would be too cumbersome to give ten minutes of dialogue here. Let's suppose that the helpee, a 22-year-old man, has been talking about his poor relationships with girls. After ten minutes of interaction, the helper summarizes:

Helper: "Let me see if I have your main points straight. First, because of your physical appearance, you think that you turn girls off before you even get to interact with them; second, you've come to expect rejection so automatically that now your initial approach to girls is hostile; and, third, this hostility is even more self-defeating because now the girls feel justified in rejecting someone who is 'mean.'
"So perhaps now you're thinking, since hostility doesn't work, that maybe it's time to search around for more constructive reactions to the unfair way you're treated."

Before doing the exercise, discuss the quality of the summary and the advanced accurate empathy in the example above.

Exercise 31: Advanced accurate empathy: An exercise in self-exploration

One way to get an experiential feeling for advanced accurate empathy is to explore some situation or issue or relationship in your own life that you would like to understand more clearly.

Directions

1. Review the sections in *The Skilled Helper* on advanced accurate empathy.
2. Read the examples given below.
3. Choose some issue, topic, situation, or relationship that you have been investigating or that you would like to take a deeper look into. Choose something that you are willing to share with your fellow trainees.
4. Briefly describe the issue (see the examples).
5. a. Write a statement that reflects a primary-level accurate empathic understanding of the issue you have chosen. This statement should reflect understanding of both your feelings and behaviors and your experiences underlying these feelings.
6. b. Write a statement that reflects your advanced accurate empathic understanding of this issue (see introduction to this section on advanced accurate empathy). This understanding should "cut deeper" into the issue.
7. Share your statements with the others in your training group. Check to see that your (b) statements are actually examples of advanced accurate empathy.

Example 1

Issue: I think that I have ambiguous feelings about people in authority. I've never explored this issue in any depth.

a. In general, I get along well with people in authority. *De facto*, I do not have run-ins with employers, police, or administrators. I feel comfortable in my conversations with them, and I can even manage some humor at times. I'm cooperative, but I also feel some satisfaction in preserving a reasonable sense of independence and autonomy in authority situations.

b. Upon reflection, even though my surface (superficial?) relationships with authority figures are calm, I believe there is some reservoir of resentment in me toward authorities, the "establishment," and so on. I find myself making jokes about them when they aren't around. I make sure that I avoid any confrontation with them, for I feel that I might be unreasonable or even irrational in such a confrontation.

Example 2

Issue: I'm concerned about the quality of my gregariousness in interpersonal and social situations.

a. I enjoy being with people. I meet people easily, and I'm generally well received and well liked. I make others feel at home. I'm outgoing and, to a degree, uninhibited when I'm with others, but I also try to be careful with others; that is, I don't want to be "too much." I think I'm genuine in dealing with others this way.

b. When I'm with people, even though I am outgoing, I'm not "all there." I don't tend to share myself deeply with others. Therefore, there is something almost superficial about my gregariousness. In my deepest moments, I am alone with myself. Perhaps I haven't learned to share my deeper self with anyone. I may even be afraid to do so. I'm not sure why.

Now do five examples from your own experience.

1. a. _____

   _____

   _____

   _____

   _____

   _____

   b. _____

   _____

2. a.

   b.

3. a.

   b.

4. a. _____

       _____

       _____

       _____

       _____

    b. _____

       _____

       _____

       _____

       _____

5. a. _____

       _____

       _____

       _____

       _____

    b. _____

       _____

       _____

       _____

       _____

HELPER SELF-DISCLOSURE

Although a helper should be *ready* to reveal anything about himself
that would help the client understand his own experience and the consequences of his behavior, he should engage in such self-disclosure only

if it is appropriate. The self-disclosure should never place the focus on the helper rather than on the client; neither, in general, should it distract the client from his work. Therefore, *what* the helper reveals about himself and the *way* in which he reveals it are both important.

Exercise 32a: Appropriateness of helper self-disclosure (in writing)

Directions

1. First, read the sections on helper self-disclosure in *The Skilled Helper*.
2. The appropriateness of helper self-disclosure depends on the entire helping context. In order to stimulate some kind of context, please return to the explanations of context and the client statements found in Exercise 29. As we assumed in that exercise, we assume here that the helper and the client have established rapport and that the client is beginning to explore his feelings, experiences, and behavior rather freely.
3. Imagine the client speaking directly to you. Then:

   a. Respond with *inappropriate* helper self-disclosure (overly dramatic, ill-timed, or distracting).
   b. Next, respond with appropriate self-disclosure—the kind that stimulates the client to understand himself from a more objective frame of reference and that will enable him to see the need for behavioral change. Try to use disclosures from your own experience; but, if you can't think of a relevant personal experience, invent something in order to get a feeling for appropriate disclosure and the manner of stating it.

Example 1 (in response to the client statement in the example for Exercise 29)

a. *Inappropriate helper self-disclosure*: "In my own life, I've found humor to be an important part of family morale. Humor has helped us through some rough times—through misunderstandings, and even through the time we had a rather serious fire at home."
b. *Appropriate helper self-disclosure*: "It's irritating to get such a different response to your humor at home. I like humor myself, but my wife once pointed out to me that family humor and my "being a wit" at home were two different things. The family, she said, appreciated the former but not the latter. I'm wondering whether anything at all similar to that is happening in your home."

Example 2 (in response to the first client statement in Exercise 29)

a. *Inappropriate helper self-disclosure*: "I had my ups and downs in graduate school. I guess we all have them. I really hated some of my courses. I went through the graduate-school syndrome, something like what you're going through now, but—well, here I am. I made it."

b. *Appropriate helper self-disclosure*: "When I went to graduate school, I hated some of the courses, and I wondered at times whether it was really worth all that effort. But I think I really wanted a graduate degree in psychology. However, what you're experiencing seems quite different. It seems that by now you have a good idea what graduate engineering is all about, but perhaps you're not quite sure that it's what you want."

Now give both inappropriate and appropriate helper self-disclosure responses to the remaining client statements in Exercise 29.

2. a. _____
    _____
    _____
    _____

    b. _____
    _____
    _____
    _____

3. a. _____
    _____
    _____
    _____

    b. _____
    _____
    _____
    _____

4. a. _____
    _____
    _____
    _____

    b. _____
    _____

5. a. _____

    b. _____

6. a. _____

    b. _____

7. a. _____

    b. _____

8. a. _____

b.   _____

     _____

     _____

     _____

9. a.   _____

     _____

     _____

     _____

b.   _____

     _____

     _____

     _____

10. a.   _____

     _____

     _____

     _____

b.   _____

     _____

     _____

     _____

Exercise 32b: Appropriateness of helper self-disclosure (face to face)

Directions

1. The training group should be divided into groups of three: helper, client, and observer.
2. The client should bring up a problem with which the helper is familiar (helper and client should be in Stage II with respect to this problem).

3. Spend five to seven minutes in a helping session, in which the helper should try to disclose himself appropriately to the client once or twice.
4. After five to seven minutes, the session should stop, and the helper should get feedback on the quality of his disclosure (with respect to both content and style) from both the client and the observer.
5. Repeat this process until each member of the group has had the opportunity to be the helper.

CONFRONTATION

Confrontation is a much-abused type of interaction in both interpersonal and helping situations. Confrontation is strong medicine and, in the hands of the inept, often destructive. Although high-level helpers do not specialize in confrontation, they do confront; but their confrontation grows organically from the helping process and is based on caring and respect. As such, confrontations are not punitive accusations but invitations to explore one's behavior, especially the discrepancies in one's life. They are invitations to employ unused strengths and resources rather than shameful unmaskings of inadequacies.

Exercise 33: Self-confrontation

Before confronting others, it is best to practice on oneself, for misguided and irresponsible confrontation can do a great deal of harm. Review the section on confrontation in *The Skilled Helper* before doing this exercise; get a feeling for both irresponsible and responsible confrontation.

Directions

Think of a few areas in your life in which you could benefit from some kind of challenge or confrontation, areas in which you should be invited to examine your behavior more carefully. Then:

a. Write out a statement in which you confront yourself irresponsibly.
b. Next, write a statement in which you confront yourself responsibly—that is, tentatively, as an invitation to self-examination.

After writing out two such self-confrontations, share them with a partner from your training group. Share how it feels to "blast" yourself, and check out the quality of your responsible confrontational statements.

Example

a. *Irresponsible*: <u>"Why don't you start being honest? You feel so damn</u>
<u>sorry for yourself most of the time that it's messing up your whole</u>
<u>life. You keep moping around, but you never really face any of your</u>
<u>problems. No wonder you're always in the dumps. You cause most of</u>
<u>your own misery."</u>

b. *Responsible*: <u>"Let me check something out with you. You're depressed</u>
<u>because, as you have put it, you 'don't do anything.' It seems that</u>
<u>sometimes you get to feeling pretty sorry for yourself. And then</u>
<u>this 'poor-me' attitude makes you even more passive and depressed.</u>
<u>Does this make sense to you?"</u>

Now confront yourself in four areas of your life, in each instance both
(a) irresponsibly and (b) responsibly.

Self-confrontation 1

a. _____
_____
_____
_____
_____
_____
_____
_____

b. _____
_____
_____
_____
_____
_____

_____

_____

Self-confrontation 2

a. _____

_____

_____

_____

_____

_____

_____

b. _____

_____

_____

_____

_____

_____

_____

Self-confrontation 3

a. _____

_____

_____

_____

_____

_____

_____

b. _____

_____

_____

_____

_____

_____

_____

Self-confrontation 4

a. _____

_____

_____

_____

_____

_____

_____

b. _____

_____

_____

_____

_____

_____

_____

Exercise 34: The confrontation round robin: Confronting and responding to confrontation

Directions

The purpose of this exercise is to give trainees an opportunity to practice both confrontation and good response to confrontation.

1. Review the general format for the round-robin experience. Also review the material on confrontation and good response to confrontation in *The Skilled Helper*.
2. Let's call the partners A and B. Partner A should (1) point out something that B does well and (2) invite B to examine some dimension of his behavior that could be improved (something that could be developed into a strength).
3. The partner being confronted (B), before responding to the confrontation itself, should indicate to A that he has understood what A is saying (accurate understanding). Only then should B proceed to explore the areas of strength and weakness suggested by the confronter.
4. Partner B then becomes the confronter, and the process is repeated with Partner A.

Unless there is some reason for not doing so, each member of the training group should have a round with every other member.

Example

Partner A: "In our group sessions, you take pains to see to it that there is a great deal of accurate empathic understanding going on. You yourself try to understand others, and you urge the other members of the group, principally by your example, to do the same. You're always genuine, and most of the time you're quite accurate.

"However, you tend to limit yourself to primary-level understanding. You're very slow to make demands on the members of the group, even when you're in the best spot to do so—for example, by using advanced accurate empathy. Your rapport is excellent, and I think you could use it to help others make more demands on themselves."

Partner B: "You see me as quite good at basic accurate empathy. It is essential in the group, and I do help provide it. However, I don't usually move beyond primary-level understanding, even though I might 'merit' doing so, since I do take such pains to understand. I should work on increasing my initiating skills."

Partner B then moves on to explore the content of his confrontation with Partner A for a few minutes.

IMMEDIACY

Immediacy refers to the helper's ability to discuss with the client what is happening in the here-and-now of their relationship and to use

88

both the relationship itself and the explicit discussion of the relationship as part of the helping process. Immediacy is dealt with last because it is a composite of skills. It ordinarily involves (1) some self-disclosure on the part of the helper, (2) some communication of advanced accurate empathy, and (3) some element of challenge or confrontation.

For instance, if the helper sees that the client is manifesting hostility toward him, but doing so in subtle, hard-to-get-at ways, he may: (1) let the client know how he (the helper) is affected by such indirect communication (self-disclosure), (2) point out the deeper messages of the client's actions and communications (advanced accurate empathy), or (3) invite the client to examine how he and the helper are relating to each other (challenge, invitation, confrontation). Immediacy, like confrontation (since immediacy includes elements of confrontation), is strong medicine and should be used carefully.

Exercise 35: Immediacy: An exercise based on your interpersonal life

Directions

1. Review the material on immediacy in *The Skilled Helper*.
2. Take a look at the examples below.
3. Think of people in your life with whom you have some unresolved or undealt-with "you-me" issues.
4. Imagine yourself talking with one of these individuals face to face.
5. Using immediacy, invite this person to deal with some issue that would enable both of you to involve yourselves with each other more creatively. Each invitation should include (1) self-disclosure of your feelings on the matter, (2) your perception of the relationship (some concrete dimension of it) as it now stands (advanced accurate empathy), and (3) an element of challenge to deal with the issue so that the relationship may grow.
6. The tentativeness that should characterize initial Stage-II interactions should be evident in your statement.

Example 1

A friend speaking to a friend:
"I find it difficult to say what I'm going to say to you. I enjoy being with you. But I feel in us—in me, at least—some kind of reluctance to share deeper concerns directly with one another. It's almost as if direct, mutual talk about our deeper concerns were forbidden territory for us. If I'm not mistaken, I think I've seen awkwardness in both of us when issues such as personal feelings about religion have come up. I wonder whether you share my perception in any way."

Example 2

A woman speaking to her husband:
"There's been no arguing between us for a month or two. It seems this might be a good time for me to bring something up. It has to do with

our style of relating to each other. It seems that when one of us gets angry with the other, the anger gets swallowed—or maybe hidden is a better word. I mean, I think the anger goes underground. Then we more or less begin to 'drift away'; I mean, we tend not to talk to each other, or to become obstructionistic in petty ways. I know I find myself almost immobilized, so that I can't even say 'Hey, what's going on between us?' I have a sneaking suspicion that the same kind of thing is happening with you. Does this make any sense to you?"

In the examples above, point out the three elements of immediacy mentioned in the introduction. Discuss the quality of the immediacy in these two examples.

Now write out three statements of immediacy dealing with people in your life outside the classroom or training situation.

1. _____

_____

_____

_____

_____

_____

_____

_____

_____

_____

_____

_____

_____

2. _____

_____

_____

_____

_____

_____

_____

_____

_____

_____

_____

_____

_____

3. _____

_____

_____

_____

_____

_____

_____

_____

_____

_____

_____

_____

Exercise 36: Immediacy: An exercise with fellow trainees

Directions

1. Review the general directions for Exercise 35.
2. Read the example below.
3. On a separate piece of paper, write out a statement of immediacy
    for each of the members of your training group. Imagine yourself
    in a face-to-face situation with each member successively. Deal
    with real, not made-up, issues.
4. In a round robin, share these statements with your fellow trainees
    (that is, share the appropriate statement with the appropriate

member) and discuss your mutual immediacy concerns for a few minutes. Continue in the round robin until you have shared an immediacy concern with and heard an immediacy concern from each of the other members of the group.

Example 1

Trainee A to Trainee B:
"I'd like to check something out with you. I have the feeling that you may resent it when I observe your helping style and give you feedback in our practice groups. As I see it, at least, it's hard for you to listen to me, because in the first few sessions here I was very heavy-handed and aggressive with you. I feel guilty about that. I think I've changed my approach, but I suspect that you may still be a bit gun-shy with me. I wonder if you see our relationship in the same way."

Example 2

Trainee B to Trainee C:
"I notice that today you haven't given me any feedback, and, in fact, that you don't give me much feedback at all. I suspect that you're trying to be gentle with me, maybe even wondering if I can 'take it.' I think you feel quite positively about me, and I appreciate your not wanting to harm me, but it may be that more direct feedback, especially from you, could help me quite a bit. If I feel that you're protecting me, then I'll feel like a child with you. And I don't want to do that. Maybe I've been a bit of a child with you already. I have to talk to you to find out whether all of this is just something I'm imagining."

Point out the elements of immediacy (self-disclosure, advanced accurate empathy, invitation/challenge) in the examples above and show how tentativeness is introduced in each. Then move on to the exercise.

Exercise 37: Empathy and immediacy

In this exercise, you are asked to review your relationship with each of the other members of your training group and to write down an immediacy concern that you think that he or she might have with you—a concern that hasn't been dealt with or hasn't been dealt with fully or adequately.

Example

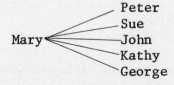

Mary reviews her relationship with each of the other members of her group. She starts with Peter and asks herself: what issues does Peter still have with me? Then she might write:

"I think that Peter has a good deal of affection for me and, perhaps some strong sexual feelings. When I am his 'client' in the practice sessions, he's very cautious with me. He tends not to give me feedback in the whole group. I believe that he would like to bring this issue out in the open but that he is hesitant to do so. Perhaps he thinks it would be inappropriate to do so, either in a one-to-one conversation or in the group."

Mary continues and writes up an immediacy issue—if she can think of one—for each of the other members of the group. These issues are then shared, either in a round robin or in a meeting of the entire group. This sharing can help build up a greater sense of community among the trainees.

Exercise 38: "Interpersonal Process Recall": An exercise in immediacy

This exercise is based on a helper-training technique, developed by Norman Kagan (in *Influencing Human Interaction*, Michigan State University CCTV, 1971), called "Interpersonal Process Recall."

Directions

1. The training group is divided into dyads—that is, helper-client pairs.
2. Each pair engages in a ten-minute helping session, using a real issue.
3. At the end of the session, each dyad meets with another dyad.
4. The helper from Dyad A meets separately with the helper from Dyad B. They help each other explore their feelings about what took place in the helping session—that is, what each helper thought and felt about himself, about the client, and about their interaction during the helping session *but did not verbalize to the client.*
5. While the two helpers are meeting, the two clients from Dyads A and B are meeting separately and doing the same thing.
6. After a few minutes of exploration, in which the members of each pair try to help each other recall the unverbalized content of the interview *as concretely as possible* (specific feelings, experiences, and behaviors), all four members of the two dyads meet together. The two members of Dyad B help the two from Dyad A share what they thought and felt during the helping interview but did not verbalize.
7. Finally, the entire process is repeated, with Dyad A helping Dyad B engage in the same process.

Note that the purpose of this exercise is to make helpers more immediately aware of what is taking place "behind the scenes" in the helping interview and to teach them to use this material immediately, in

93

the here-and-now of the interview itself. In other words, this exercise constitutes *immediacy* training.

Study the following examples before engaging in this exercise.

Example 1

The following statement is the kind that the helper in Dyad A might share with the helper in Dyad B after the helping interview with the trainee-client:

"I felt myself getting tense, and I noticed that my palms were sweating, because I thought that I was having difficulty responding accurately to the client. I even had the suspicion that the client was being almost deliberately evasive. I was getting angry, but I was trying to ignore my anger and pretend that everything was all right. As a result, I became increasingly preoccupied with myself. This self-consciousness affected my ability to listen to the client."

Example 2

The following statement is the kind that the client in Dyad A might share with the client in Dyad B after the helping interview with the trainee-helper:

"I saw that, if I were really going to come to grips with my interpersonal life, I was going to have to talk about my sexual behavior. All of a sudden I said to myself 'You're in too deep for a training session.' I got scared. My pulse shot up, and I began to talk about all sorts of unconnected interpersonal experiences just to stay clear of the area of sex. I felt that the helper and I were both stumbling around, but that I wanted it to be that way at the moment."

Example 3

The following are examples of the kinds of statements the trainee-helper and trainee-client might share with each other after they have conferred with trainee-helper and trainee-client, respectively, from the other dyad:

Helper in Dyad B to client in Dyad B: "I felt trusted by you when you told me that it was evident that you should ask your father to talk about what you see as an oppressive unwritten contract for your living at home while you go to school. When you described how afraid you are to talk to him, you seemed to let your uneasiness about the situation—including the guilt you feel for cutting yourself off from him—flow into your nonverbal behavior. You showed it in your tone of voice and in your hesitancy. It seemed you trusted me enough to let it flow, and your trust made me more confident."

Client in Dyad B to helper in Dyad B: "Yes, I felt myself relaxing with you, even though I was talking about being uptight with my father. When you suggested that I seemed to be trying to talk myself into facing him squarely with what I see as an unlivable home situation, I felt that you had drawn a legitimate conclusion from what I was saying, but I still

94

felt pushed. I still trusted you, but I began to see you as someone who was going to put demands on me, and I felt myself tightening up."

Finally, helper and client talk about whether sharing these thoughts and feelings *during* the helping interview itself might have helped.

PUTTING IT ALL TOGETHER IN STAGE II

You are asked to integrate the skills of Stage I and the skills of Stage II in the following exercise.

Exercise 39: Counseling oneself: An exercise in Stage-II skills

Directions

1. In this exercise (which is similar to Exercise 28, except that it deals with Stage II skills as well), you are asked to write out a dialogue with yourself.
2. Choose a problem area that has already been developed in Stage I (perhaps the same one you dealt with in Exercise 28). The problem area should be relevant to your interpersonal style and/or competence as a helper.
3. Use the skills of Stages I and II (but especially those of Stage II) to help yourself explore the problem further and come to the kind of self-understanding that demands action (although it is not necessary to elaborate an explicit action program).
4. First, study the following example. Then, with a partner,

    a. Identify the kinds of responses the helper uses (such as primary-level accurate empathy, advanced accurate empathy, confrontation, or immediacy).
    b. Criticize the manner in which the helper proceeds (the quality of his responses).
    c. Suggest more effective responses, if you think they are called for.

Context: The person in the following example has been discussing the painful disorganization and lack of discipline in his life. He feels anxious, lacking definite purpose, and pulled in many directions. He has examined a number of areas of disorganization and has focused on his disorganized interpersonal life.

Self: I've always thought that I should be as free as possible, but getting involved with people immediately cuts down on my freedom. I don't think that's the way I want it. For instance, the girl I'm going out with now is beginning to put more demands on me. She expects me to be the one to take her places. She just won't allow our relationship to remain unstructured.

Response to self: She's getting to you where you feel it the most—in your sense of freedom.

Self: She's not the first one. This is the third or fourth time this has happened. I've said good-by to two other girls because they began to make these kinds of demands on me. Now it's starting all over again.

Response: You come to feel constricted in your relationship with each girl, but it seems that she looks at the relationship differently. It sounds almost as if you and the girl are not contracting for the same thing from the beginning.

Self: I believe they get to the point where they want to own me, and I don't want to be owned by anybody.

Response: Are you saying that you would like intimacy without ties or interpersonal demands? If so, that might be a pretty tall order.

Self: Oh, hell, I can set up any kind of interpersonal system I want. If others don't like it, they don't have to get involved with me.

Response: So, in your present relationships, involvement pretty much means involvement on your terms. If others don't want it that way, well, they can just move on.

Self: I don't need a lot of moralizing about my behavior. Morality is different today. People relate differently today. I don't need anyone to monitor my behavior.

Response: It almost sounds as if you're saying that you don't need me butting into your business. Perhaps I'm doing now what the others do: infringing on your freedom.

Self: Well, I think you're implying that I'm not free to set up my own rules in relationships, and I don't want to believe that's true.

Response: Maybe I am implying that. It could be that I'm even implying that it's kind of hard for you to set up your own rules to govern *our* relationship. I guess I'm beginning to place demands on you to take a look at the consequences of setting up rules unilaterally. And I think this is hard work for both of us.

Self: I really am touchy about my freedom. In fact, as I talk to you here, it probably seems that I'm defining myself by my freedom. I don't think I like your implying that all relationships demand more give and take than I'm ready for. Even my relationship with you here. I suppose I sound pretty selfish to you.

Response: To see your own behavior as others see it is painful for you—something you've preferred to avoid.

Self: But I've paid the price for avoiding it. That's why I'm here.

5. After reviewing the helper's responses above, write a dialogue with yourself, using a combination of Stage-I and Stage-II interactions that will help move yourself toward action.

SECTION 8
RATING SCALES

Table 2

HELPING BEHAVIORS: A RATING SCALE

1	/	1.5	/	2	/	2.5	/	3	/	3.5	/	4	/	4.5	/	5
extremely poor		poor		inadequate		minimally facilitative		good		extremely good		excellent

STAGE-I SKILLS

Primary-level accurate empathy: the helper communicates an accurate understanding of the feelings, experiences, and behaviors of the client from the client's frame of reference.

Concreteness: the helper helps the client speak about concrete and specific feelings, experiences, and behaviors in specific situations. He encourages relevant disclosure rather than storytelling.

Genuineness: the helper is always himself; he is not phony; he doesn't hide behind professional roles, he is spontaneous and open, but he doesn't overwhelm the client with himself; he is nondefensive.

Respect: the helper's verbal and nonverbal behavior indicate that he is "for" the client, working for his interests. He is initially nonjudgmental but, gradually, he helps the client place demands on himself; he shows regard for the individuality and the resources of the client.

STAGE-II SKILLS

Advanced accurate empathy: the helper communicates an understanding of what the client only implies, what he hesitates to say, or what he has poorly formulated; he helps the client understand himself at deeper levels.

Self-disclosure: the helper is ready to disclose anything about himself that will enable the client to understand himself better, but he actually discloses himself only when it will help rather than distract the client; he discloses himself in a way that keeps the focus on the client.

Confrontation: the helper challenges discrepancies in the client's life and in the client's communication with the helper; he invites him to explore these discrepancies; he challenges the client to employ unused resources.

Immediacy: the helper talks about what is happening between himself and the client in the here-and-now of their relationship, as a way of helping the client explore his interpersonal style and of helping him see himself from alternative frames of reference.

STAGE-III SKILLS

Directionality: the helper directs the client's attention to "choice points" in his life; he helps him elaborate behavioral-change strategies and action programs; he teaches the client the basic principles of the maintenance and change of behavior. He also teaches the client problem-solving methodologies and helps him apply them to the concrete problems of his life.

Behavioral support: the helper uses Stage-I and Stage-II skills to provide both support and challenge for the client as he works through behavioral-change programs. He encourages, supports, reinforces, and confronts.

THE TRAINEE AS AGENT IN THE TRAINING PROCESS

In order to become an *agent* in the training process itself, you must continually examine your proficiency in each of the skills required for effective helping. This worksheet is meant to help you "prime the pump" of agency within you.

Rate yourself on the following skills:

Skills   *Week*

Attending

Accurate empathy
   (primary-level)

Communication of
   respect

Communication of
   genuineness

Concreteness

Accurate empathy
   (advanced)

Self-disclosure

Immediacy

Confrontation

Elaboration of
   action programs

Concreteness in
   action programs

Use of principles
   of behavioral
   change

Behavioral
   Support

Which of these skills need more work on your part?

How active are you in seeking feedback from both the trainer and your fellow trainees?

What do they say in their feedback?

State your strengths and your deficiencies as concretely as possible. For example: What parts of the attending process give you trouble? Which principles of behavioral change do you ignore or misuse?

What is your immediate behavioral program for making yourself more proficient in these skills? What must you do within the training sessions themselves? What must you work on outside the training sessions?

99

SECTION 9
RESPONSES TO SELECTED EXERCISES

Since most of the exercises in this manual do not deal with absolutely right or wrong responses, the responses listed in the following pages are suggested responses, not the correct answers. In some cases, the trainee's response may be better than the one listed here. Responses should fulfill the demands of the helping model, but they should also reflect the individuality of each trainee. Trainees should compare their responses with those listed here to determine which seem more effective.

Exercise 14: Responses

1. b, e, g, i, j, k
2. b, d, f, g, h
3. a, c, g, h
4. d, e, h
5. c, e, f, g, i, k
6. c, d, f, g, h,
7. a, d, e, f, i
8. c, d, e, h, i
9. a, b, c, d, h, j, k
10. e, i, j, k

Exercise 15: Responses

1. a, d
2. c, d
3. a, b
4. d, e
5. b, d
6. a, c, e
7. b, d
8. a, b, c
9. b, d
10. a, c

Exercise 16: Some possible responses

1. miserable, angry, resentful, abused, humiliated, ridiculed, upset

2. not great but okay, grateful, at peace, fairly content, "making it," fairly well satisfied, putting up with it, confident, independent

3. furious, angry, enraged, outraged, offended, mistreated, abused, picked on, despised

4. puzzled, perplexed, confused, uncertain, on edge, jumpy, nervous, anxious, helpless, irritated, annoyed, in doubt

5. cautious, hesitant, anxious, reluctant, justified, tense, uncertain, wondering, curious, apprehensive, fragile

6. happy, warm, friendly, open, delighted, gratified, surprised, enthusiastic

7. torn, disappointed, resentful, hurt, angry, helpless, in a bind, confused, upset, disheartened, frustrated

8. unsettled, disappointed (in self), trapped, in a bind, guilty, ineffective, uncomfortable, flat, marking time, directionless, defeated

9. (cautiously) optimistic, growing in confidence, pleased, moving ahead, growing, confident, grateful, gratified, glad, sure, contented, determined

Exercise 17: Some possible responses

Note that these responses are suggestions, not the definitively correct answers.

1. her classmates seem so smug and insensitive
    her classmates are making fun of her

2. she is getting adequate care
    complaining is not her "style"

3. the police barge in like strangers who don't really give a damn
    the police are insensitive, and they do more harm than good

4. he doesn't know how to deal with his boss
    working with an inconsistent boss seems to be too much for him
    to take

5. he thinks he might be pressured into revealing too much of himself
    he is not sure what is going to be demanded of him, especially in
    terms of self-disclosure

6. she has had such a great time
    he has been thoughtful, yet so much fun

7. her husband refuses to face her illness with her
    her husband doesn't seem to realize that he is alienating her and
    causing her pain

8. she hates her work and yet is not open to a change of jobs
    the work is unengaging and joyless, but a change might be too
    disruptive

9. he is learning how to be a caring yet independent person
    he has found out that he can be a good helper without being loved
    by every client

Exercise 18: Some possible responses

1. embarrassed, out of place, mortified, like slipping away unnoticed

2. isolated, lonely, a bit depressed

3. surprised, amazed

4. resentful, angry, victimized, caught, bitter

5. cautious, hesitant, doubtful, puzzled

6. uneasy, anxious, apprehensive, scared

7. annoyed, irritated, taken advantage of, second-rate

8. relieved, pleasantly surprised, glad

9. reluctant, embarrassed

10. overwhelmed, at the end of your rope, like you've had it, fed up,
    under tremendous pressure

11. panicked, frightened, under the gun, like you just can't do it

Exercise 19: Some possible responses

1. you weren't prepared for so formal a party

2. your loved ones are gone and retirement gives you a lot of time on
    your hands

3. he actually stuck to his part of the bargain

4. she's following the same pattern, this time using her illness to
    place demands on you

5. it's not yet clear whether he's interested just in himself or in
    you as a person

6. no one has taken the time to let you know what you're getting into

7. you're always asked to play second fiddle to her

8. he actually treated you as if you were a human being!

9. it's just too private to share in a first meeting with someone

10. the committee's probing your status simply compounds all the pressure you're under right now

11. you think you'll just make a fool of yourself in front of the whole class

Exercise 20: Some possible responses

1. satisfied and dissatisfied
   contented and bored

2. resentful and appreciative
   irritated and wanted
   pressured and cared about

3. disappointed in yourself and determined
   embarrassed and ready to fight

4. fed up and challenged
   discouraged and fulfilled

5. angry and guilty
   justified and ashamed

6. vulnerable and misused
   defenseless and taken advantage of

7. mistreated and capable
   angry and confident in yourself

8. pleased and apprehensive
   pleasantly surprised and anxious

9. loving and at your wits' end
   appreciated and victimized

10. lonely and discouraged
    isolated and helpless

Exercise 21: Some possible responses

2. You feel both appreciative and irritated because, even though people here like you, they are making what you see as unreasonable demands on you.

3. You feel embarrassed by having to ask for help, but you're also determined and ready to fight because you still want to be the master of your own ship.

4. You're fed up with the crap you have to take from these kids, but you also feel challenged, because this kind of work makes you put out everything you've got.

5. In one sense you're glad you got back at the little brat, but you also feel guilty, because blowing up like that didn't really solve anything or help anyone.

6. You feel vulnerable because you're ready to give in to him on almost everything, but you also feel mistreated and abused because he's taking advantage of you.

7. You're angry because they haven't been playing fair with you, but you feel good about yourself because you see yourself as an effective helper and realize that you don't have to stick to the ministry in order to help.

8. Although you feel pleased that *you* were chosen from the secretarial pool, you're nevertheless apprehensive, because this job is going to place new and unknown demands on you.

9. You feel grateful and loving because he *is* a good husband to you, yet you're exasperated because he's making life unbearable for you in the neighborhood.

10. You feel both isolated, because these are new people and different from you, and discouraged, because you can't seem to make contact with them.

Exercise 22: Some possible responses

2. a. You feel angry with yourself because you knew you were riding for a fall but went ahead anyway.
   b. It sounds as if you'd like to kick yourself in the ass. You kind of let yourself act stupidly, and now you're really caught.

3. a. You feel proud of yourself and your initiative because you were smart enough to get hold of yourself before it was too late.
   b. It's great to look back and see that you practically lifted yourself up by your own bookstraps—you were in the pit one year and riding high the next.

4. a. You feel terrified because the next seven months seem to promise a worse hell than the one you're in now.
   b. The thought of being locked on board for seven months is intolerable. You're really desperate to get off the ship.

5. a. You're angry because the pain is getting to you and we seem unconcerned, and because we abandon you.
   b. Not enough medication and being ignored when you need us most must really seem awful to you.

104

6. a. You're fed up and you feel abused because people won't let you live down an impulsive mistake.
   b. It's really unfair to be made to pay for the same mistake over and over. That's worse than the mistake itself.

7. a. You feel resentful because you don't think I'm being fair and honest with you.
   b. You see me as putting you down unfairly and not being honest, and you resent that.

8. a. You feel embarrassed because you were so uptight you just froze.
   b. You just froze up so completely that you couldn't do anything about it. And you probably feel a little sheepish about it now.

9. a. You feel caught because she holds the purse strings.
   b. She's got you where she wants you. It seems you can't do anything about it.

10. a. You feel bad because you've missed the opportunity of reviewing the plus factors in your life for so long now.
    b. You've just never thought of yourself as a capable person, and that's depressing. It looks as if a census of your strengths and resources is long overdue.

Exercise 23: Some possible responses

2. a. You feel depressed because that kind of rejection just isn't easy to take, and you're also quite anxious, wondering how you're going to handle it.
   b. You've dreaded this moment, and now it's here; it looks very depressing. You also sound as if you're at your wits' end wondering how to handle it.

3. a. You're infuriated because of what he did to your sister, and yet you feel some compassion, because he's not an evil person, and he's your brother.
   b. Conning your sister and upsetting the whole family—that's the last straw. And yet I think you're wondering how you can deal harshly with a brother who isn't really an evil person.

4. a. You feel relieved just to get it off your chest straight and honest, but you're still in a bind, because telling someone doesn't decrease your desire to drink.
   b. It feels good to come clean like this with someone, but, in a sense, you can say "What's the use?" There's something fatalistic about it—you feel you're still going to drink.

5. a. You feel ashamed because you hurt her, and yet you're frustrated because she won't let you speak to her directly.
   b. Talking about her behind her back wasn't the answer. It blew up in your face. But not being able to level with her is just too frustrating.

6. a. You feel relatively at ease because the semester is over, but you're actually still uptight thinking about the courses for next semester.
   b. You sound like you're still on the battlefield—there's only a lull between battles.

Exercise 27: Responses

1. a. Minus   cliché
   b. Minus   irrelevant, distracting, closed question
   c. Minus   premature advice
   d. Minus   premature confrontation

2. a. Minus   inadequate response, no response at all
   b. Minus   *inaccurate* empathy
   c. Minus   premature advanced accurate(?) empathy
   d. Plus

3. a. Minus   irrelevant, distracting, closed question
   b. Minus   premature confrontation
   c. Plus
   d. Minus   inappropriate or premature helper self-disclosure

4. a. Minus   lack of respect, rejection
   b. Minus   inaccurate empathy
   c. Minus   inappropriate or premature immediacy
   d. Minus   distracting statement that ignores the problem

5. a. Plus
   b. Minus   premature or inaccurate advanced empathy
   c. Minus   cliché
   d. Minus   inappropriate, distracting helper self-disclosure

6. a. Minus   inadequate response, nonresponse
   b. Minus   inappropriate warmth
   c. Minus   rejection, lack of respect
   d. Minus   premature immediacy

7. a. Minus   inappropriate sympathy or warmth
   b. Minus   judgmental
   c. Minus   premature action program or advice
   d. Plus

8. a. Minus   judgmental; premature (and possibly inaccurate) confrontation
   b. Minus   inappropriate warmth, perhaps patronizing
   c. Minus   inappropriate self-disclosure
   d. Minus   closed, irrelevant question

9. a. Minus   premature or inaccurate advanced empathy
   b. Minus   rejection, lack of respect
   c. Minus   inaccurate primary-level empathy
   d. Plus

10. a. Minus   cliché
     b. Minus   placating, patronizing
     c. Minus   rejection, lack of respect
     d. Minus   inappropriate (premature, inaccurate, unverifiable)
                       empathy

Exercise 29: Some possible responses

Share your responses with the members of your training group. Compare your responses with those given here. See if you can improve on the responses given here.

1. a. You're disappointed—in the school, in some of the teachers, and maybe even in your own lack of enthusiasm.
    b. It's been a very disappointing time. Perhaps disappointing enough to wonder whether engineering is the right choice for you.

2. a. Life was once very full, but it seems pretty empty now; that's hard to face.
    b. I hear your loneliness, but it seems that I might also be hearing a note of self-pity. It's almost as if you were intimating that life is all over now.

3. a. You feel out in left field when she clicks off like that, and you'd like to make sense out of what's going on.
    b. It's unsettling not to know what's going on. You begin wondering whether she's just moody or, perhaps, whether your style at times makes her click off like that.

4. a. You have a certain "what's the use?" feeling. Showing up here alone and telling the story once again doesn't really change anything.
    b. Telling *her* story becomes more and more frustrating. If she needs to punish you, perhaps we should try to find out what you do that she thinks must be punished. That might give us another angle to work with.

5. a. It's certainly disappointing not to be chosen, but you feel you don't have the right to be *too* disappointed.
    b. When you reason things out, one part of you says that you have no right to be very upset. Yet there seems to be another part of you that says "I *am* upset; I *am* disappointed; I *am* angry."

6. a. It's pretty bleak when work—which is more or less your life—loses its appeal, at least for the present.
    b. Is it conceivable that you're beginning to think that a life that is all work already has a kind of bleakness about it, and, perhaps, that "freely" choosing to work all the time is not exactly the freedom it seems to be?

7. a. When you look at the whole picture, it's practically too dismal for words.

b. The negative things in your life seem to be sitting on you like a rock; it might seem almost useless for you to take a census of resources and possibilities.

8. a. You feel caught. You're afraid of losing your daughter's respect, but you don't want to give up your freedom, either.
   b. It sounds as if you're in a kind of dilemma. You're not sure whether your daughter will approve of your behavior. On the other hand, you're not very interested in changing the way you relate to men. Perhaps it's a little hard to put these two factors together.

9. a. It feels great to let your spirits soar for a while. It gives you a better perspective on life.
   b. I may be wrong, but it seems to me that, when your spirits soar like this, it makes you wonder whether your day-to-day life is more drab than it has to be.

10. a. Despite some ups and downs, you're pretty satisfied with your relationship with your mother.
    b. John, as I listen to you, I think I may also hear you saying that it might be a good idea to examine a little more care-fully the impact your mother has on your wife and family. Are you hinting at that at all?